Matthew
My mum for always encouraging me, and my children,
Sam, Ophelia, Keanu and Iman.

Justin and Louise
To our mums and dads, William and Sally Gellatly
and Roy and Pamela Reynolds.

FIG TREE

UK | USA | Canada | Ireland | Australia
India | New Zealand | South Africa

Fig Tree is part of the Penguin Random House group of companies
whose addresses can be found at global.penguinrandomhouse.com.

Penguin
Random House
UK

First published 2017
001

Copyright © Matthew Jones, Justin Gellatly and Louise Gellatly, 2017
Photography copyright © Issy Croker
Lammas Day photography copyright © Al Richardson, pages 17, 59, 63 and 64–5
Historical photographs on chapter openers copyright © Getty Images,
pages 28, 56, 66, 100, 124, 168, 190, 206, 226, 242, 258, 276 and 294

Printed in China

A CIP catalogue record for this book is available from the British Library

ISBN: 978–0–241–28518–3

www.greenpenguin.co.uk

BAKING SCHOOL

THE BREAD AHEAD COOKBOOK

MATTHEW JONES, JUSTIN GELLATLY
AND LOUISE GELLATLY

PHOTOGRAPHY BY
ISSY CROKER

PENGUIN
FIG TREE

THE BREAD AHEAD STORY

At Bread Ahead we simply love baking, cooking and eating.

Bread Ahead started in September 2013, when Matt Jones was offered amazing premises at Borough Market to start a new bakery. Matt had been baking for years, first in restaurants, then founding Flour Power City Bakery in 1999, and he asked Justin Gellatly to be his head baker. Justin had been baking for the previous decade at St John Restaurants and St John Bread and Wine, and, luckily for Bread Ahead, Justin's wife, chef Louise Gellatly, came too.

With just three of us, we began our days at 3 a.m. and baked merrily away to produce breads and other delights for our stall at Borough Market. Back then, we didn't even have a kitchen porter, so at the end of a long shift we had to wash up and clean everything before starting work again (none of us miss that now!). As time went on we started to supply bread to local restaurants within Borough Market. In February 2014 we opened the school and started our baking classes, then we took on another baker, a teacher and a couple of kitchen porters and never looked back. Today we have a team of over twenty bakers, seven teachers and ten kitchen porters, and there are Bread Ahead bakeries in four more London locations as well as our Borough Market bakery school and stall. On the wholesale side of things, there are over 100 restaurants and hotels that depend on us for their daily bread, and we are now teaching over 300 students a week. It's certainly turned into a busy little bakery!

We have learned over the last three years from our pupils exactly what people want to learn at a bakery school, and this book reflects the courses that we run: Baking Techniques, Sourdough Baking, Flatbreads, Puff Pastry, Doughnuts, and our wonderful regional baking course – English, Italian, French, American, Nordic, Eastern European and Great British Baking – as well as a terrific Gluten-free Baking course.

We originally planned to run two groups of twelve people a week at Bread Ahead, so Matt called up an old friend who used to work for him, Emmanuel Hadjiandreou, a fellow baker and teacher; we invited our friends and family to the school and taught them how to make bread, and in the process we developed the structure and format of our teaching and classes.

Things kicked off fairly quickly, with classes being booked up months in advance, so it was time to bring in another teacher full-time – and we were lucky to find Master Baker Aidan Chapman, who really helped us develop the Bread Ahead school and its classes.

A couple of years down the line, we now run about 25 different classes, 7 days a week. We needed a head teacher, and again we were very lucky to find Master Baker Manuel Monade, whom both Matt and Justin had baked with before. We now all teach in the school, which the three of us really love, and we are always encouraging our bakers to think about teaching as well.

In the bakery school, we just use domestic kit, including the ovens – we use Miele ovens, which we think are the best – so everything we teach can be brought back to the comfort of your own kitchen.

We now regularly teach over 300 people a week, and in addition to this we work with local schools and run education packages for the next generation of bakers.

We also have Barry Cummings, our other full-time teacher, who has decades of experience within the baking world, as well as many guest teachers including Sim Cass, star baker of the famous Balthazar Bakery in New York, Adriana Rabinovich, who is at the forefront of gluten-free baking, and Hilary Cacchio, a real sourdough expert.

And we are looking forward to many more people teaching at Bread Ahead in the future.

INTRODUCTION

We have written this book as a practical, realistic guide for bakers at all levels. We like to see our approach to baking as modern, unfussy and as simple as possible. We use natural, honest ingredients and, above all, concentrate on creating deep, satisfying flavours, the sort of food that is a truly memorable experience. When it comes to our range of breads, we stick to simple recipes and develop natural, robust flavours. We achieve this with long fermentation and bake at high temperatures to get a rich crust with plenty of singe . . . and it is all about that crust!

Though we run a bakery, this book is all about baking at home. With these recipes, we will show you what can be achieved with some very basic household equipment and a generous amount of enthusiasm and commitment.

We have developed and tested these recipes at home, with the attention to detail that will deliver consistent reliability for all your baking needs. This is a book for everyone: whether you want to master the perfect sourdough, or simply whip up some flatbreads for friends one evening. We will take you on an educational journey and give you a deeper, richer understanding of modern baking. We want you to love baking in the same way we do.

The book is divided into chapters based on the courses that we run at the Bread Ahead Baking School, from regional baking (British, French, Italian, Eastern European, and so on), to techniques for sourdough, puff pastry, our famous doughnuts, and much more besides. We would like to fill your hearts, kitchens and homes with the same glorious smells that pour out on to Cathedral Street each day and night from our place down at London's Borough Market.

Happy baking!

Matt, Justin and Louise

FIVE BASIC RULES OF BAKING

At the end of the day, really good baking requires experience and practice, along with discipline, good work ethics, consistency, planning and commitment. At Bread Ahead we have been at it for a while now, so here are five basic rules that will help you get the results you dream of.

1 / TEA
Don't start baking without a cup of tea, an apron, a nice tidy kitchen and the radio on.

2 / KNOW YOUR MILLER
Try not to chop and change when it comes to flour and other basic ingredients. To achieve consistency it's imperative that you use the same flour each time, as you need to get a feel for the flour and develop a relationship with it. After a while you will get to instinctively know the moisture content and structure.

At Bread Ahead we use Marriage's flour. Marriage's is a family-run company that has been milling since 1824 and is based not too far away from the bakery, in Chelmsford, Essex. We have a close relationship with Marriage's, as quality is at the heart of what we do, and it's important to us that they still use British wheat, which they mill themselves.

3 / DON'T WORRY IF IT IS A TOTAL DISASTER FIRST TIME AROUND
It's all relative. Rarely is a loaf totally inedible.

Baking is a lifelong journey – try to see it this way, and remember that it gets easier with practice.

When you're supplying 100 restaurants, 7 days a week, you can't afford to make mistakes, so enjoy it at home if things don't go quite to plan – nobody's going to tell you off!

4 / EVERY LOAF IS DIFFERENT
Artisan baking is a bit temperamental by nature at times. Get used to this.

Much as we are looking for a certain level of consistency in what we do, baking can also involve (and you should expect) a certain level of inconsistency. If you can get your head round this concept, you are well on the way to being an artisan baker.

5 / SOME THINGS ARE HARDER THAN OTHERS

It's a good idea to start off with something easy in order to get to know our approach and the way we do things – our language, if you will. Starting off with a notoriously tricky sourdough on day 1 wouldn't be recommended for a beginner – go for a batch of scones to go with that cup of tea we mentioned earlier, and enjoy yourselves.

BAKING: THE ELEMENTS

In this first section we'll look at essential ingredients, what they do, and why things happen. Much as we like to think of baking as an artistic and creative endeavour, it really helps to have a grasp of the basic laws of biology and chemistry.

So, without being overly scientific, we have set out here to 'demystify' some of the seemingly overwhelming fundamentals of baking. By understanding these principles we are leaving less to chance, and, by mastering the basics, we actually gain more freedom in what we are able to do.

When baking using yeast-based products, we are working with a living, breathing culture that requires a very specific set of conditions to exist in. Pastry also has its own set of rules, though the two are quite different in temperament.

Good bakers instinctively know what to look for in dough texture, temperature and so many of the other variables that affect what they do. For the home baker, who might bake only once or twice a week, these things will come with time, but here are some facts to help you on the way.

YEAST

Yeast is so much more than just an ingredient – think of it as a way of adding life to your dough. Dried and fresh yeast are both good for home baking, but will always take second place to the natural or wild yeast found in our sourdoughs.

The benefits of fresh yeast are its active nature and 'baker friendliness'. It's available in most large supermarkets these days (ask in the bakery section) and can be kept in the fridge at home for 2–3 weeks, ideally at 1–4°C. In most artisan bakeries you will find fresh yeast as well as several live cultures.

Dried yeast keeps for longer and is a perfectly good alternative to the fresh stuff. It's slightly slower acting, but this is no bad thing.

Yeast snobbery – there are some purist bakers who frown on both fresh and dried yeast. We take the view that when used sparingly and under the correct conditions, fresh yeast is invaluable to what we do.

People have been baking with yeast for thousands of years – it's mentioned in the Bible, and depicted in hieroglyphs left by the ancient Egyptians. Looking from a scientific perspective at what our forebears were doing thousands of years ago with the most basic of tools, little has changed. What has changed massively are our basic ingredients, our tools and our environment. Yeast has always simply done, and will always do, the things it knows best – among these is its ability to convert carbohydrates/sugars into carbon dioxide, which produces the essential air pockets in our bread.

We won't get too bogged down at this stage with yeast strains and complex science, so for simplicity let's keep 'baker's yeast' (i.e. dried or fresh rather than wild yeast) in mind. We will explore sourdoughs and wild yeasts in their own separate chapter.

Like all living things, yeast ('culture' is the collective noun for yeast cells) requires some basic conditions to exist in. A bread dough at a temperature of between 10°C and 24°C is a perfect place for yeast to become active. Most essentially, it needs a food source and warmth in which to function.

It's important to remember that once the sugars have all been consumed from a dough, the yeast will run out of food and die. The temperature range will also dramatically affect the yeast's activity – cooler is slower, to a point where 0°C is almost no activity, and above 27°C the cells will start to die off.

SALT

Salt is vital to making great bread, for several reasons. The first is flavouring – but it does much more than this.

The second role salt plays is in slowing down the yeast's activity. Salt draws water from the yeast, which means it develops more slowly. Bread dough without salt will very quickly over-prove.

Third, salt strengthens your dough, making it more elastic and building a better structure. This helps to create the air pockets where the CO_2 from the yeast forms, as well as helping to form a stronger, crisper crust. Be careful when measuring out your salt, though, as too much salt will kill the yeast and leave you with a dead dough. Putting salt into contact with the yeast directly will also kill it.

Once in a while we forget to put salt in a batch of bread; this is about as bad as it gets in the midst of a busy production schedule – when you're halfway home, and you start thinking, 'Did I put that 620g in that last mix . . . did I . . . didn't I?'

Basically, this spells disaster – in-the-bin, start-all-over-again kind of disaster. Once your dough has started to prove, adding the salt is not usually an option, as the dough will become overworked, breaking down the delicate texture.

There is just no mistaking the taste of the dreaded 'forgotten salt bread' – it's awful. It has a strange, bitter aftertaste, and really is unpleasant to eat. So don't forget your salt. It will be a total nightmare if you do.

We use two types of salt at Bread Ahead – fine and coarse/flaky. They are both unrefined, additive-free natural sea salts. Fine sea salt is required for dough-making, as it dissolves fairly quickly and will get fully and evenly mixed throughout your dough in a relatively short time. Coarse sea salt flakes are for sprinkling on top of focaccia and other breads and bakes.

Have a look at the packet labelling and go for something along the lines of 'unrefined natural sea salt'. What you want to avoid is anything with an anti-caking agent.

WATER

In my experience, bakers use tap water for every recipe. In our case, good old London Thames tap water. There will be differences across the country – harder/softer, etc. – but we have found these have no noticeable impact on either the flavour or the performance of our recipes.

Commercial and artisan bakeries alike generally have water meters that dispense measured amounts of water at a precise temperature. This is especially important when mixing large quantities, as the machine produces a lot of friction, which in turn will heat up the dough. With this in mind, it's common for bakers to use ice-cold water in order to end up with a dough that reads at 16°C when mixed.

It's worth noting that when mixing your dough, you need to bear in mind the temperature of the other ingredients as well as the environment you are working in.

Ideally the water temperature should be between 25°C and 35°C. If the water is very cold, adjust it with a little warm water, and, if it's a bit warm, adjust it with some cold water or a little ice.

With the recipes in the book, we have used cold water straight from the tap unless otherwise stated, and **we always weigh the water in grams.**

GLOSSARY OF BAKING TERMS

Remember these – some recipes in the book will use them, plus you can sound like a professional baker down the baking club.

FERMENTATION TERMS

BIGA – Italian kind of 'sponge' (baking term meaning a pre-ferment). A biga is a quantity of flour and water, mixed with fresh yeast and made the day before your dough, which gives the dough a nice depth of flavour. A biga can be held longer at its peak than a wetter sponge such as a poolish (opposite).

LEVAIN – As per sourdough, this is the traditional French term for both the starter and the sourdough bread.

OLD DOUGH/VIEILLE PÂTE – A piece of dough left over from the last batch and added to the next dough, which will improve the flavour of the loaf.

POOLISH – The French version of a biga, and with a wetter 'sponge' (another word for a pre-ferment). It's usually equal quantities of flour and water, mixed with fresh yeast and made the day before your dough, giving the dough a nice depth of flavour.

PRE-FERMENT/SPONGE/STARTER – A mix made the day before baking (or more), added to the final dough to help improve the flavour and extend the life of the loaf.

REFRESH – To feed, generally the starter, with more water and flour, an essential part of the process of feeding the yeast cells, otherwise they will exhaust their food supply and eventually die.

RETARD – To slow down the process of fermentation by cooling the dough; yeast activity slows down considerably as the dough cools. At 2.5–5°C it is almost hibernating and retarding, whereas at 24°C+ it's off to the races.

STARTER/WILD YEAST/MOTHER/SOURDOUGH CULTURE/LEVAIN – A mixture of flour and water plus wild yeast, left to ferment over 5–6 days, and fed continually with more flour and water.

YEAST – We always use fresh yeast at the bakery; if using dried yeast, halve the amount. You can find fresh yeast online, or in health food shops, and it is widely available in Polish supermarkets. Often bakeries in the larger supermakets will sell it to you too.

OTHER BAKING TERMS

BAKING STONE – Made of ceramic or stone and placed on the bottom rack of the oven, a baking stone will retain heat and will transfer this heat to your loaf for a better bake and crust.

BANNETON/PROVING BASKET – Cane, wicker, plastic or wood baskets are used for proving the shaped loaf, holding the shape of the dough to keep it from spreading out.

BLOOM – The opening of the crust during baking.

COUCHE – A heavy linen fabric (you can use a tea towel), used to hold shaped loaves for proving. The fabric can be folded round the loaves to help them hold their shape.

CRUMB – The texture of the inside of the loaf (i.e. not the crust).

DUTCH OVEN – A cast-iron or ceramic pot with a lid, used to emulate the baker's oven so that the bread will self-steam inside. A Le Creuset style casserole works well.

ENRICHED DOUGH – Dough that has been 'enriched' with butter, egg and sugar. This inhibits the yeast, which is why brioche and croissants need lots of yeast.

HYDRATION – The water content of the dough. A 100% hydration is 1kg each of flour/water, for example; 80% hydration is 800g of water and 1kg of flour.

LAME – The blade used to score the dough (we use razor blades on a handle).

PEEL – A thin piece of wood or metal with a handle to help slide the loaf into the oven.

PRE-SHAPE – To relax the dough, so it's easier to shape, and persuade the gluten in the flour to perform better when shaping.

PROVING – The final rest period before baking, after the dough has been shaped and is in its basket or couche.

SPRITZER – A water spray used to inject water into the oven to produce steam.

MAKING YOUR BREAD

'STRETCHING AND TEARING'

WET DOUGH (PAGE OPPOSITE)

'Poised like a puma' (your hand in a claw shape resting above the dough), with the heel of your hand push the dough into the work surface and 'stretch and tear' the dough forwards, then grab it and bring it back to where you started the 'stretch and tear'. Repeat for the required length of time stated in the recipe. Make sure you scrape your dough to the centre throughout the 'stretch and tear' process to make sure it gets developed evenly. After a few minutes you should be able to feel the start of development in the dough.

STIFF DOUGH

'Poised like a puma', with the heel of your hand push the dough into the work surface and 'stretch and tear' the dough forwards. You will need to hold on to the end of the dough to do this, then grab it and fold it back over itself. Repeat for the required length of time in the recipe, again making sure you scrape your dough to the centre throughout the 'stretch and tear' process to make sure it gets developed evenly. After a few minutes you should be able to feel the start of development in the dough.

FOLDING THE DOUGH

Folding is one of the best ways of incorporating air and encouraging gluten development in any dough. Gluten development creates more tension in the dough, which means you are more likely to get the 'oven spring' that results in a taller loaf. The more developed the gluten strands are in your dough, the stronger and more elastic they will be, meaning they are easier to work with and more likely to trap bubbles of air to create a better 'crumb' in your finished loaf. Here's how to fold your dough:

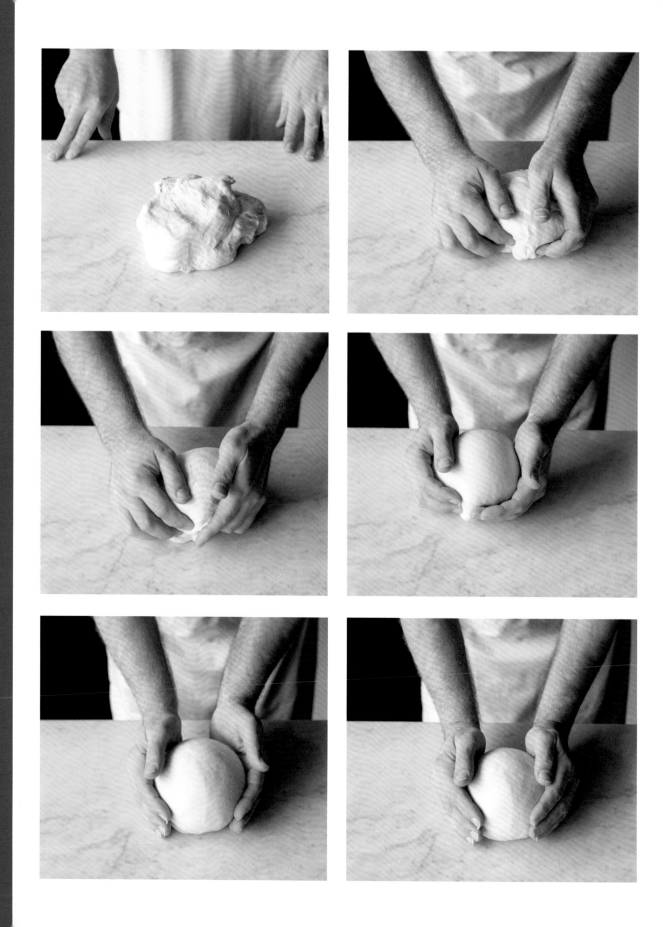

- First, pick up the top two corners and pull up, stretching the dough upwards, then fold over to the opposite side (the first corners should meet the opposite two corners).

- Next, pick up the bottom two corners and again pull up, stretching the dough up and over, and fold to the opposite side.

- Now repeat for the left- and right-hand sides, then flip the whole of your dough over, so that the bottom becomes the top.

SLAPPING THE DOUGH

Using one hand, grab the centre of the dough and lift it about 30cm into the air, then slap it down on to the work surface with a flat hand. Repeat for the required length of time stated in the recipe, making sure you scrape the dough to the centre throughout the slapping of the dough, to make sure it gets developed evenly. After a few minutes you should be able to feel the start of development in the dough.

MIXING

Most of the recipes in the book are done by hand. As we tell our bakers, HANDS LEARN – they will feel the changes in the dough during the mixing, as the gluten develops, and it's more fun to use your hands too. Plus you transfer your love into the dough.

However, with all our recipes you can dust off your mixer, if you have one, and use that. The timings remain the same.

SHAPING THE DOUGH

We have tried to make this as simple as possible, so as not to put you off loving shaping your loaf.

When using extra flour for dusting, you have to be careful not to overdo it for two reasons:

- It will give you pockets of raw flour through the dough.
- The dough will be harder to shape.

So first, try it without any flour, then, if you are having trouble, just dip your hands in the flour once and clap any excess off.

PRE-SHAPE

The easy way is to cup your hands and tuck the sides of the dough underneath until your hands meet, then rotate the dough clockwise, repeating the tuck, and rotate until a full circle is reached. It doesn't need to look pretty.

ROUND/BALL (PAGE 20)

Turn the dough upside down, grabbing the sides of the dough and bringing them into the middle. This will bring tension to the dough. Flip it over and repeat the pre-shape motion (above), then pop it into a floured proving basket or on to a baking tray, seam side up. Alternatively, you can repeat the pre-shape technique until you have a nice smooth firm ball. It should feel like a firm bosom or buttock.

BAGUETTE (PAGE OPPOSITE)

Grab the dough with both hands, one on either side, then gently stretch it out to form a rough rectangle. Take the top of the dough, fold it over tightly with your thumbs, then repeat that action until you reach the end of the dough and seal the bottom together. If the end hasn't sealed, just pinch the dough together, then lay it in your couche (see page 16), seam side up.

LONG/TIN (PAGE 24)

Take the dough with both hands, one on either side, then gently stretch out the dough to form a rough rectangle. Take the top of the dough, fold it over tightly with your thumbs, then bring in the two sides and fold over with your thumbs again. Repeat until you reach the end of the dough, then with the heel of your hand seal the seam together and place seam side up in your proving basket, or seam side down for tins.

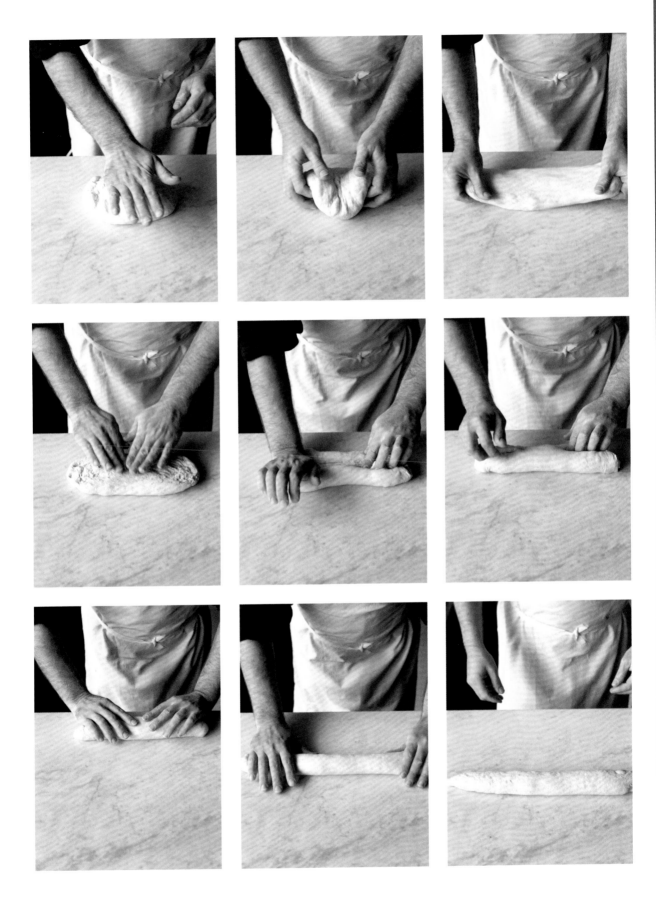

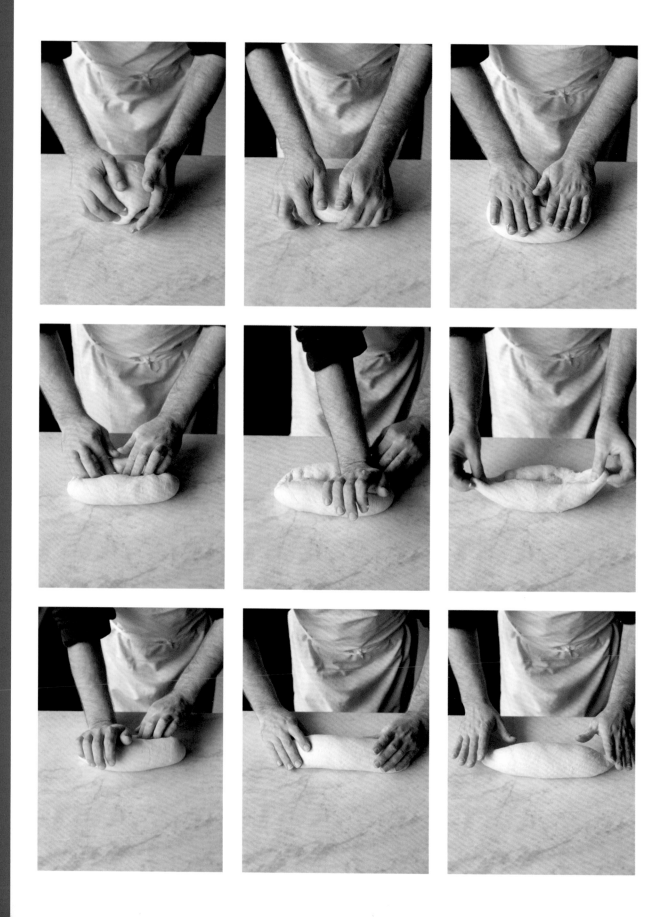

STICK

First roll a sausage shape, then with both hands flat and with equal pressure, start to roll from the centre of the dough, moving your hands slowly but firmly along the length of it, rolling as you go, to form a stick.

PLAIT

Cut your dough into 3 equal pieces and roll them into even lengths. To do this, first roll a sausage shape, then with both hands flat and with equal pressure, start to roll from the centre of the dough, moving your hands slowly but firmly along its length, rolling as you go, to form a strand. Now, to plait: with the 3 strands in front of you, squidge the 3 ends together, then position them 10cm apart from each other (but connected at the top). Take the right-hand strand and cross it over the middle strand (so the right-hand strand becomes the middle), then take the left-hand strand across the middle strand and repeat until the end is reached. Squidge the ends together and place on a baking tray lined with baking paper.

BUN/DOUGHNUT

Take a piece of dough the desired weight, then with one hand take your blob of dough, form a claw with your hand and place it over the dough. Push down, applying some pressure so that you are touching the dough with your palm. Now, in a circular rolling motion, move the dough round the 'cage' of your clawed hand, making sure you are applying pressure to the dough so tension is formed. Keep rolling until a smooth, tight, round ball is achieved.

+ THE BAKER'S TOOLBOX +

DUTCH OVEN	**PASSION**	PIPING BAGS
BOWLS	DEEP-FAT FRYER	SIEVES
PATIENCE	WATER SPRAY	BAKING TRAYS
SCRAPER	DIGITAL SCALES	BAKING PAPER
ROLLING PIN	BAKING STONE	PROVING BASKETS
WHISKS	BLADES	COUCHE
MEASURING SPOONS	PEEL	**LOVE**
LOAF TINS	SAUCEPANS	THERMOMETER
COOLING RACKS	**SENSE OF HUMOUR**	OVEN GLOVES OR MITTS
TIMERS	SPRINGFORM CAKE TIN	BOX GRATER
SHOWER CAPS	WOODEN SPOONS	HANDHELD GRATER (IDEALLY MICROPLANE)
CLING FILM	TEA BAGS	
PASTRY CUTTERS	PASTRY BRUSH	**TIME**

DUTCH OVEN (CAST-IRON CASSEROLE)

This is our favourite way of baking bread at home, and we really encourage you to do the same. To test the recipes we used the following:

- For a large loaf, we used an oval pot 25cm x 33cm x 14cm deep.

- For a medium loaf, we used an oval pot 20cm x 26cm x 10cm deep.

- For a small loaf, we used a 19cm round pot 9cm deep.

SOURDOUGH BAKING

ourdough is our bread and butter at the Bread Ahead bakery (pun intended). We are very serious about the sourdough movement, and the largest part of our production in the bakery is white and brown sourdough loaves. We send our sourdough all around London every morning, baking over 1,000 kilos of it every day.

The sourdough loaf is all about a long fermentation, the development of a real depth of flavour, the open texture of the crumb, a chewy leathery crust, plus a nice singe and a flavour that sings.

Bakers have been baking using sourdough techniques since ancient Egyptian times. It's the natural way to bake bread, and it's only in the last 100 years, since the mass production of commercial yeast and those ever-increasing fermentation shortcuts, that sourdough has been left behind.

Over the last fifteen years the sourdough revolution has become massive, and has led to people rediscovering ancient grains and the techniques of long fermentation, and most importantly bringing flavour, crust and character back to our loaf. It has brought many new people into baking, which is fantastic, and it has helped the baking revolution really kick off, with small and micro sourdough bakeries opening up all over the place.

One of the main reasons many of our bakers come to work at Bread Ahead is to learn the ways of the Bread Ahead Sour. In the Bread Ahead Baking School we get many chefs and bakers coming into our 3-day sourdough class to learn how to make sourdough, carrying the movement further. We also run free demos at Borough Market, showing people how to make their own starter.

It's important to relax about your sourdough starter – all you need is flour, water and time, plus the right conditions, which you can control! Don't forget to name your starter, as it will become part of the family – our starter at Bread Ahead is called Bruce, after Canon Bruce Saunders, who was the first clergyman to bless our bread at Southwark Cathedral.

CARING FOR YOUR STARTER

WHAT IS A SOURDOUGH STARTER (AKA 'MOTHER')?
A sourdough starter is used to cultivate wild yeast in a form that we can use for baking. Since wild yeast is present in all flour (and in the air), the easiest way to make a starter is by combining flour and water and letting it sit for several days.

WHICH FLOURS CAN I USE TO MAKE A STARTER?
You can use any flour to make a starter, but we recommend using a wholegrain rye flour (and we use this in our production bakery). Rye starters tend to be a bit heartier and more resilient than their white counterparts.

HOW LONG DOES IT TAKE TO MAKE A STARTER?
It should take about 6 days to create a healthy, bubbly starter. By this point, your starter should have a honeycomb pattern of bubbles in it and a slightly alcoholic aroma.

HOW/WHERE SHOULD I KEEP MY STARTER WHEN I'M MAKING IT?
During these first 6 days (when you're feeding and growing your starter), it should be kept loosely covered at room temperature.

HOW/WHERE SHOULD I KEEP MY STARTER AFTER THE FIRST 6 DAYS?
If you're not baking with your starter straight away, put it into the fridge, with the lid of the container firmly fastened. If you're not baking regularly with your starter, you'll need to give it a feed (50g of flour and 50g of water) every 2 weeks.

WHAT IF I'M GOING ON HOLIDAY FOR MORE THAN 2 WEEKS?
You can freeze your starter. Once you're ready to use it again, allow it to defrost at room temperature, and feed it daily (50g of flour and 50g of water) until it's back to its bubbly self (this may take a few days).

WHAT HAPPENS IF LIQUID APPEARS ON TOP OF MY STARTER?
Don't worry if this happens – it's harmless and is referred to as 'hooch', which is naturally occurring alcohol. It's basically your starter saying 'I

am hungry' and 'FEED ME'. The hooch can either be poured off or mixed back into your starter – we are 'hooch in' at Bread Ahead.

HOW DO I KNOW WHEN MY STARTER IS NO LONGER RESCUABLE?

If your starter begins to smell like dirty nappies, or the result of a night on the Brussels sprouts, it's time to throw it away and start again. Simply give it a stir (it will probably have a sizeable layer of hooch on it by this point in time), then transfer 50g to a new container (discard the rest) and feed it daily with 50g of water and 50g of flour until it's bubbly and ready to use.

ONCE I'VE DECIDED TO BAKE A LOAF OF BREAD, WHEN AND HOW MUCH SHOULD I FEED MY STARTER?

Once you decide you're going to bake a loaf of bread, you'll need to feed your starter 8–12 hours before you bake (if you're using a wholegrain starter you'll need to feed it at least 8 hours before; if you're using a white starter, you'll need to feed it at least 12 hours before). Take a look at your recipe, and if it calls for 150g of starter, feed your starter with 75g of flour and 75g of water so that the total volume of added ingredients is 150g. Then leave your starter out at room temperature, covered loosely, until you're ready to use it.

WHAT SHOULD I KEEP MY STARTER IN?

This largely comes down to personal preference. Kilner jars are a popular option, but we've kept very healthy starters in plastic pots for years without any problems.

HOW MUCH STARTER SHOULD I GENERALLY KEEP?

Again, this largely comes down to personal preference, but we recommend keeping about 500g.

WHAT IS THE DIFFERENCE BETWEEN A STARTER AND A STIFF STARTER?

So from the rye starter we make our stiff starter – from Bruce to Son of Bruce. We use this stiff starter in many of our sourdoughs at Bread Ahead, feeding daily over 500kg. The main difference is, as the name suggests, that it is stiffer – with more flour and less water being used it is easy to handle, especially on a large scale. It still gives you a lovely depth of flavour for your sourdough – it's really a matter of personal preference.

RYE STARTER

DAY 1

50g wholegrain rye flour

50g cold water

DAYS 2, 3, 4 & 5

1 tablespoon wholegrain
rye flour

1 tablespoon cold water

On day 1, just mix the flour and water together. Cover with a tea towel and leave at room temperature for 24 hours.

Each consecutive day, add 1 tablespoon of flour and 1 tablespoon of water to your existing starter, and mix. By day 5 it should be nice and lively, with some bubbling and a slightly alcoholic aroma.

Store in the fridge in an airtight container and use at least once a fortnight. Before use, feed with 75g of rye flour and 75g of water (or whatever volume your recipe requires) and leave at room temperature for 8 hours.

STIFF STARTER

Feed your rye starter a good 8 hours before you make this so that it is nice and lively.

85g strong white
bread flour

43g water

42g rye starter
(see above)

Put the flour, water and starter into a bowl and mix until combined.

Cover with cling film or a shower cap and leave at room temperature for 8–14 hours.

BREAD AHEAD SOURDOUGH

This is the first loaf of bread we made and baked at Bread Ahead, in September 2013. We think we baked about 20 loaves, and now we are in the thousands every day.

It is a joyous loaf with great flavour and crust, and pretty much goes with anything, as a sandwich or a vehicle for other foods, but the flavour never gets lost and always sings.

Put the starter and the water into a large bowl and begin to break up the starter into smaller parts by squeezing it through your hands – which is oddly satisfying!

Now add the flours, then, with one hand shaped like a fork, gently bring everything together until just combined, which should take only a couple of minutes. Scrape the dough off your hand into the bowl, then take the dough out of the bowl and place it on a floured work surface, making sure you scrape all the dough out with a scraper to leave a clean bowl. Keep the bowl to one side, as you will need it later.

Now, with your dough on the work surface and you 'poised like a puma' (see page 18), with the heel of your hand push the dough into the work surface and 'stretch and tear', using the technique described on page 18, for about 6 minutes. After 4 minutes you will begin to feel the dough strengthen as the gluten develops. Scrape the dough back into the bowl you used earlier, and leave to rest for 20 minutes.

Scrape the dough back on to your work surface. Add the salt to the dough and, again 'poised like a puma', start to gently bring the salt into the dough for a couple of minutes, making sure you mix it through evenly, as you don't want pockets of salt in the dough.

Lightly oil the bowl, pop the dough back in, then give your dough a fold using the technique described on page 21. After folding, leave it to rest for an hour, then give the dough three more folds, resting for an hour each time. Between folds, you will need to cover the bowl with cling film, a tea towel or a shower cap. After the final fold, leave the dough for another hour. Please don't stress if you end up missing a fold or your timing goes out of sync – always remember that bread-baking is a journey and one you should enjoy.

MAKES I LARGE LOAF

145g stiff starter
(see page 33)

400g water

400g strong white
bread flour, plus extra
for dusting

50g wholemeal flour

50g rye flour

12g fine sea salt

oil, for the bowl

semolina, for dusting

YOU WILL NEED
a Dutch oven
(cast-iron casserole)
or a baking stone

a water spray

a baker's peel or
a wooden board

After the last rest, take your proving basket and a clean tea towel. Fold the towel in half, lay it in the basket and lightly sprinkle it with wholemeal flour. Pop the loaf, bottom side up, into the lined proving basket and cover with a shower cap. Place in the fridge for about 8–12 hours, or overnight, so that the fermentation carries on slowly.

Next day, take the dough out of the fridge and leave it for 1 hour before uncovering. Don't forget to give it a smell – it should have a gorgeous wheaty and sour aroma.

Preheat your oven to 250°C/fan 230°C/gas 10, or as hot as it will go. Once it's ready, pop a Dutch oven (cast-iron casserole) or baking stone into the oven to heat up for about 10 minutes. Get your water spray ready if using a baking stone.

If using a Dutch oven, very carefully take it out of the oven. Sprinkle the dough with semolina and gently place it top side down in the Dutch oven, then, using a sharp knife or a razor blade, cut two slashes in the top. Put the lid on and bake for 35 minutes, then remove the lid and bake for a further 25 minutes.

Take the Dutch oven out and very carefully remove the loaf, then pop the loaf back into the oven, directly on the oven shelf, and bake for a further 5–10 minutes, depending on how much singe you like.

If using a baking stone, gently and slowly turn out your dough on to a baker's peel or a wooden board, then, using a sharp knife or razor blade, cut two slashes in the top. Slide it on to the baking stone in the oven, then heavily spray the inside of the oven with your water spray and bake for 30 minutes.

After 30 minutes, turn the tray round and bake for a further 25 minutes, depending on how much singe you like.

Once baked, place on a rack to cool.

THE LOAF
By Mr and Mrs G

Baker, bring me a loaf
A loaf of beauty
Not just in beauty, filled with flavour
The flavour of love (and fermentation)
My loaf of love, from the fire
With crust of singe, the staff of life

THE MICHE

A miche is simply a rounded loaf; we always give it a hard bake at the bakery so the crust gives the crumb a run for its money on taste. You will see these in bakeries all around France, generally large ones about 2½kg, which people buy as their bread for the whole week.

On day 1, mix the water and starter together, then mix in the flour. Cover with a tea towel or shower cap and leave overnight at room temperature.

Next day (day 2), weigh out the water, add the overnight ferment and mix together to combine.

Place your flours in a large bowl and combine with one hand, just enough to let them get to know each other, then make a well in the centre.

Pour the water mix into the bowl of flour, then, with one hand shaped like a fork, gently bring together until just combined. Scrape the dough off your hand into the bowl, then take the dough out of the bowl and place it on a work surface, making sure you scrape all the dough out with a scraper to leave a clean bowl. Keep the bowl to one side, as you will need it later.

Now, with your dough on the work surface and you 'poised like a puma' (see page 18), with the heel of your hand push the dough into the work surface and 'stretch and tear', using the technique described on page 18, for about 8 minutes. Scrape the dough back into the bowl you used earlier, and leave for 20 minutes.

Scrape the dough back on to your work surface, add the salt, and, again 'poised like a puma', start to 'stretch and tear' to gently bring the salt into the dough, just for a couple of minutes, until incorporated evenly.

Lightly oil your bowl and pop the dough back in, then give it a fold using the technique described on page 21. Leave it to rest for an hour, then give the dough three more folds, resting for an hour each time. Between folds you will need to cover the bowl with cling film, a tea towel or a shower cap. After the final fold, leave it for another hour.

Now take a large proving basket and line it with a clean tea towel – fold the towel in half, lay it in the basket and sprinkle

MAKES I MIGHTY LOAF

DAY I: THE OVERNIGHT FERMENT

150g water

100g rye starter
(see page 33)

200g wholemeal flour

DAY 2

780g water

300g strong white
bread flour

700g wholemeal flour,
plus extra for dusting

20g fine sea salt

oil, for the bowl

semolina, for dusting

YOU WILL NEED

a baking stone

a water spray

a baker's peel or
a wooden board

lightly with wholemeal flour. Gently take your dough out of the bowl and put it on a floured work surface. Gently shape it into a ball, then put the dough top side down in the lined proving basket and cover with a shower cap. Either leave to prove for 3 hours, or put it back into the fridge overnight for extra fermentation.

Preheat your oven to 250°C/fan 230°C/gas 10, or as hot as it will go, and place a baking stone in to heat up. Get your water spray ready.

If you went for an extra night in the fridge, go straight from fridge to oven. Either way, you are ready to bake. Sprinkle a baker's peel or a wooden board with semolina and very gently and slowly turn out your loaf on to it. With a sharp knife or a razor blade, slash several cuts on top of the loaf, then slide it off the peel on to the baking stone in the oven. Heavily spray inside the oven with your water spray, and bake for 30 minutes.

After 30 minutes, turn the miche round and bake for a further 30 minutes, depending on how much singe you like.

Once baked, place on a rack to cool.

RAISIN AND HONEY SOURDOUGH

This is perfect on the cheeseboard, as the flavour of the loaf really stands up to strong cheeses. We like it best served with a strong, heady goat's cheese, but it's also very good with butter and jam.

On day 1, put the raisins into a bowl with the water, cover and leave overnight.

Next day (day 2), strain the raisins and put to one side, but keep the strained raisin water and top up the weight to 300g. Add the rye starter to this raisin water and mix together until combined.

Place your flours in a large bowl and combine with one hand, just enough to let the flours get to know each other, then make a well in the centre.

Pour the water mix into the bowl of flour, then, with one hand shaped like a fork, gently bring together until just combined. Scrape the dough off your hand into the bowl, then take the dough out of the bowl and place it on your work surface, making sure you scrape all the dough out with a scraper to leave a clean bowl. Keep the bowl to one side, as you will need it later.

Now, with your dough on the work surface and you 'poised like a puma' (see page 18), with the heel of your hand push the dough into the work surface and 'stretch and tear', using the technique described on page 18, for about 4 minutes, making sure you scrape all the dough to the centre so that it gets developed evenly. Scrape the dough back into the bowl you used earlier, and leave for 20 minutes.

Scrape the dough back on to your work surface, then add the soaked, drained raisins, honey and salt to the dough. Again 'poised like a puma', start to 'stretch and tear' to gently bring the raisins into the dough, just for a couple of minutes. Try not to be too hard on the dough – you want the raisins to turn into pockets of joy throughout the loaf, and not to break down to mush.

Lightly oil your bowl, pop the dough back in, then give it a fold using the technique described on page 21. After folding,

MAKES 2 BAGUETTE STYLE LOAVES, WHICH WILL GIVE YOU SMALL SLICES PERFECT FOR CHEESE

DAY 1

160g raisins

160g water

DAY 2

the raisin soaking liquid, made up to 300g with extra water

80g rye starter (see page 33)

365g strong white bread flour, plus extra for dusting

55g wholemeal flour

15g honey

8g fine sea salt

oil, for the bowl

semolina, for dusting

YOU WILL NEED

a baking stone

a water spray

a baker's peel or a wooden board

leave to rest for 30 minutes, then give the dough two more folds, resting for 30 minutes in between. Between folds you will need to cover the bowl with cling film, a tea towel or a shower cap. After the final fold, leave it for 1 hour. Please do not stress if you end up missing a fold or your timing goes out of sync – always remember that bread-baking is a journey and one you should enjoy.

When the hour is up, pop the dough into the fridge for about 8–12 hours, or overnight, so that the fermentation carries on slowly.

Next day, take the dough out of the fridge and leave it for 1 hour before uncovering. Don't forget to give it a smell – it should have a gorgeous, yeasty, sweet and sour aroma.

The dough should have firmed up, so gently take it out of the bowl and pop it on a lightly floured work surface. Gently shape the dough into a round, then cover with a tea towel and leave to rest for 15 minutes to relax the dough.

OK, now, with the dough and yourself relaxed, shape it into 2 baguettes (see page 22). Remember they must fit into your oven – so don't make them too long!

Place the first baguette on a floured cloth with the seam side up, then bring the cloth up round it and place the next one directly alongside – the weight of each dough piece will help hold the shape. Now leave them to prove for 2 hours if you want to bake them today; alternatively you can prove them for 1 hour then pop them into the fridge until you are ready to bake.

Preheat your oven to 220°C/fan 200°C/gas 7 and put a baking stone in to heat up. Get your water spray ready.

Sprinkle a baker's peel or a wooden board with semolina, then very gently and slowly take out one baguette and place it on the peel (no slashing for this loaf). Slide it off the peel on to the baking stone in the oven, then repeat with the second baguette. Heavily spray inside the oven with your water spray. Bake for 20 minutes, then turn the baguettes round and bake them for a further 10 minutes.

Once baked, place on a rack to cool.

FENNEL, SUNFLOWER AND PUMPKIN SOURDOUGH

We bake hundreds of these beauties every day in the bakery. The deep fennel flavour goes really well with cured meats, and also makes amazing croutons.

Put all the seeds into a deep roasting tray and roast in the oven at 180°C/fan 160°C/gas 4 until deep golden brown. Or you can mix the seeds together in a bowl, then fry them on a medium heat on the hob, using a large frying pan, again to a deep golden brown. Put them into a bowl and leave to cool, then cover with 200g of water and leave, covered, overnight.

Next day, strain the soaked seeds and put to one side, reserving the strained soaking water. Top up the soaking water to 400g. Add the stiff starter to your water/soaking liquid, and start to break up the starter into smaller parts by squeezing it through your hands – which is oddly satisfying!

Put your flours into a large bowl and combine with one hand, just enough to let the flours get to know each other, then make a well in the centre. Pour the liquid into the flour, then, with one hand shaped like a fork, gently bring together until just combined. It should take only a couple of minutes. Scrape the dough off your hand into the bowl, then take the dough out of the bowl and place it on your floured work surface, making sure you scrape all the dough out with a scraper to leave a clean bowl. Keep the bowl to one side, as you will need it later.

Now, with your dough on the work surface and you 'poised like a puma' (see page 18), with the heel of your hand push the dough into the work surface and 'stretch and tear' for about 6 minutes, using the technique described on page 18. After 4 minutes you will begin to feel the dough strengthen as the gluten develops. Scrape the dough back into the bowl you used earlier, and leave for 20 minutes.

Scrape the dough back on to your work surface, add the roasted seeds and the salt, and again 'poised like a puma' start to gently 'stretch and tear', to bring the seeds and salt into the dough, just for a couple of minutes. Make sure you don't have pockets of seeds – you want to mix them through the dough evenly.

MAKES A PRETTY LARGE LOAF, ENOUGH FOR THE WHOLE FAMILY

10g fennel seeds

100g sunflower seeds

80g pumpkin seeds

10g linseeds

400g water, including the soaking water from the roasted seeds (see method)

150g stiff starter (see page 33)

375g strong white bread flour, plus extra for dusting

50g wholemeal flour

50g rye flour

12g fine sea salt

oil, for the bowl

plus some extra unroasted seeds for dipping the dough in before baking

semolina, for dusting

Lightly oil your bowl, pop the dough back in, then give it a fold using the technique described on page 21. After folding, leave to rest for an hour, then give the dough three more folds, resting for an hour each time. Between folds you will need to cover the bowl with cling film, a tea towel or a shower cap. After the final fold, leave it in the bowl for another hour.

Fold a clean tea towel in half, lay it in your proving basket, and lightly sprinkle it with wholemeal flour. Get ready a tray with your dusting seeds on and a shallow tray with some water in it.

Shape your dough into a nice, smooth, tight round (see page 22) and dip it into the water, covering the dough. Then roll the dough in your tray of seeds and literally carpet bomb it with seeds to cover it completely.

Put the rounded loaf, bottom side up, into your lined proving basket and cover. Now pop the dough into the fridge for about 8–12 hours or overnight, to slowly carry on the fermentation.

Next day, take the dough out of the fridge and leave it for 1 hour before uncovering. Don't forget to give it a smell – it should have a gorgeous, yeasty, nutty and sour aroma.

Preheat your oven to 250°C/fan 230°C/gas 10, or as hot as it will go.

Once your oven is ready, pop a Dutch oven (cast-iron casserole) or a baking stone into the oven to heat up for about 10 minutes. Get your water spray ready if using a baking stone.

If using a Dutch oven, very carefully take it out of the oven. Sprinkle the loaf with semolina and gently place it top side down in the pan. Put the lid on, place in the oven and bake for 35 minutes, then remove the lid and bake for a further 25 minutes. Take out the Dutch oven and very carefully remove the loaf, then pop the loaf back into the oven, directly on the oven shelf, and bake for a further 10 minutes, depending on how much singe you like.

If using a baking stone, gently and slowly turn out your loaf on to a baker's peel or a wooden board. Slide it off the peel on to the baking stone in the oven. Heavily spray inside the oven with your water spray and bake for 30 minutes, then turn the tray round and bake for a further 30 minutes.

Once baked, place on a rack to cool.

YOU WILL NEED

a Dutch oven (cast-iron casserole) or a baking stone

a water spray

a baker's peel or a wooden board

NO KNEAD SOURDOUGH

At Bread Ahead, we believe everyone can fit great bread-making into their lives. This no knead sourdough recipe is perfect no matter how busy a schedule you have, and it produces an amazing loaf.

MAKES A HAPPY
1KG LOAF

500g strong white
bread flour, plus extra
for dusting

150g rye starter
(see page 33)

350g water

11g fine sea salt

semolina, for dusting

YOU WILL NEED

a Dutch oven
(cast-iron casserole)
or a baking stone

a water spray

a baker's peel or
a wooden board

DAY 1: Place the flour in a large mixing bowl. In another bowl, add the starter to the water and mix (your starter should float in the water). Make a well in the centre of the flour and pour in the liquid.

With your hand like a fork, gently bring the dough together (don't overmix – at this stage you just want to combine until the flour has cleared). Cover and leave at room temperature for 1 hour.

In this recipe, we use the delayed salt method. This gives your starter time to become active and your flour time to absorb water before the salt is added.

When the hour is up, uncover your dough and place the salt on top. Sprinkle a little water over the salt, then gently start pulling the salt through the dough. This should take about 30 seconds, at which point you should feel your dough start to tighten up slightly.

Cover your dough and place in the fridge for 12–24 hours.

DAY 2: Take your dough from the fridge and uncover. It will be a lot firmer now and will be starting to resemble a fully mixed dough.

You now need to give your dough a fold, using the technique described on page 21. This will start to develop the gluten, reactivate the yeast and put air pockets into the dough. Rest it for half an hour, then give it another fold. Rest for another half hour, then take your dough out of the bowl and give it a gentle pre-shape (see page 22). Cover and leave for 10 minutes.

Heavily dust your proving basket with flour, then shape your dough into a nice tight round by bringing the outside edges of your hands together (palms facing up) underneath the loaf as you turn it on your work surface. This will create good tension in the loaf.

Place the dough upside down in the proving basket and leave to prove for 1 hour at room temperature. Cover and place in the fridge for another 8–12 hours.

DAY 3: Take your dough out of the fridge and leave it to rise for about 2 hours.

Preheat your oven to 250°C/fan 230°C/gas 10, or as hot as it will go.

Once your oven is ready, put a Dutch oven (cast-iron casserole) or baking stone in to heat up. Get your water spray ready if you are using a baking stone.

If using a Dutch oven, very carefully take it out of the oven. Sprinkle the loaf with semolina and gently place top side down in the Dutch oven. Using a razor blade, cut two slashes in the dough. Put the lid on, place in the oven and bake for 35 minutes, then remove the lid and bake for a further 25 minutes.

Take the Dutch oven out and very carefully remove the loaf, then put it back into the oven, directly on the oven shelf, and bake for a further 10 minutes, depending on how much singe you like.

If using a baking stone, gently and slowly turn out your loaf on to a baker's peel or a wooden board. Using a sharp knife or a razor blade, cut two slashes on the top of the loaf, then slide it off the peel on to the baking stone in the oven. Heavily spray inside the oven with your water spray, and bake for 30 minutes.

After 30 minutes, turn the loaf round and bake for a further 25 minutes, depending on how much singe you like.

Once baked, place on a rack to cool.

CATHEDRAL/CHAPEL LOAF

This is our mammoth loaf, named after our neighbours at Southwark Cathedral, where we made our sourdough starter, which was blessed there too (see Lammas Day, page 57). Unless you have a commercial-size deck oven, you will need to scale down this recipe to produce its smaller brother, the Chapel loaf. Quantities for both are provided below.

Put the starter and water into a large bowl and begin to break up the starter into smaller parts by squeezing it through your hands – which is oddly satisfying!

Add the flour and salt, then, with one hand shaped like a fork, gently bring everything together until just combined – it should take only a couple of minutes. Scrape the dough off your hand into the bowl, then take the dough out of the bowl and place it on a floured work surface, making sure you scrape all the dough out with a scraper to leave a clean bowl. Keep the bowl to one side, as you will need it later.

Now, with your dough on the work surface and you 'poised like a puma' (see page 18), with the heel of your hand push the dough into the work surface and 'stretch and tear', using the technique described on page 18, for about 8 minutes. After 4 minutes, you will begin to feel the dough strengthen as the gluten develops.

Lightly oil the bowl you used earlier and put the dough back in, then give it a fold, using the technique described on page 21. After folding, leave it to rest for 1 hour, then give it one more fold and rest it for another hour. Between folds you will need to cover the bowl with cling film, a tea towel or a shower cap. After resting the dough for an hour following the second fold, cover again and place in the fridge for about 8–12 hours, or overnight.

Next day, take the dough out of the fridge and uncover. Don't forget to give it a smell – it should have a slightly sour aroma. The dough should have firmed up overnight, so gently take it out of the bowl and pop it on a floured work surface. Gently shape the dough into a round (see page 22), then cover with a tea towel and leave to rest for 15 minutes, to relax the dough.

THE CATHEDRAL

MAKES A LOAF ABOUT 1 METRE LONG, WHICH IS WHY WE SELL IT IN PIECES AT BREAD AHEAD

1.24kg stiff starter (see page 33)

2.4kg water

3.3kg strong white bread flour

64g fine sea salt

oil, for the bowl

semolina, for dusting

THE CHAPEL

SERVES THE WHOLE FAMILY

155g stiff starter (see page 33)

300g water

415g strong white bread flour, plus extra for dusting

10g fine sea salt

a Dutch oven
(cast-iron casserole)
or a baking stone

a water spray

a baker's peel or
a wooden board

Now press the dough out to form a rectangle. Form a lip along the top, then tuck your dough in, making it as tight as you can and rolling it out into a longer shape. Remember, though, that it must fit into your oven, so don't make it too long. Either place it seam side up on a floured cloth and wrap the cloth round it, or put it into a floured long proving basket. Cover and leave to prove for about 3 hours.

Preheat your oven to about 250°C/fan 230°C/gas 10, or as hot as it will go.

Once your oven is ready, pop a Dutch oven (or cast-iron casserole) or baking stone into the oven to heat up for about 10 minutes. Get your water spray ready if you are using a baking stone.

If using a Dutch oven, very carefully take it out of the oven. Sprinkle the loaf with semolina and gently place it top side down in the Dutch oven, then, using a sharp knife or a razor blade, cut three crosses on top of the dough, down the middle and at either end. Put the lid on, put it back into the oven and bake for 45 minutes, then remove the lid and bake for a further 10 minutes. Take the Dutch oven out of the oven and very carefully remove the loaf, then pop the loaf back, directly on the oven shelf, and bake for a further 10–15 minutes, depending on how much singe you like.

If using a baking stone, gently and slowly turn out your loaf on to a peel or a wooden board. With a sharp knife or a razor blade, cut two crosses on top of the dough, down the middle and at either end, then slide it off the peel on to the baking stone in the oven. Heavily spray inside the oven with your water spray, and bake for 30 minutes.

After 30 minutes, turn the loaf round and bake for a further 25 minutes.

Take out of the oven and place on a rack to cool.

100% RYE SOURDOUGH

Does exactly what it says on the tin! This thick-crusted loaf with a moist crumb will sit happily in your bread tin for 2–3 weeks (if it lasts that long). It's one of our favourite loaves and is perfect for making open-faced sandwiches. It also makes delicious, crunchy and interesting croutons.

Feed your starter a good 8 hours before you make the pre-ferment, so it is nice and lively.

On day 1, mix the starter and water together in a bowl, then combine until all lumps are broken up (a whisk is handy for this). Add the flour and bring together to form a nice loose mixture. Cover and leave at room temperature for 12–24 hours.

Next day (day 2), uncover your pre-ferment. It should have lots of air bubbles in it and have a pleasant, slightly alcoholic aroma.

Add the water to the pre-ferment and again mix until all the lumps are broken up. Mix in the salt, followed by the flour, then, with one hand shaped like a fork, bring the mixture together and continue mixing for a good 2 minutes until fully combined.

Pat down the dough with a floured hand to smooth the top, then sprinkle with flour. Cover and leave for 1 hour to ferment and rest.

Fold a clean tea towel in half and lay it in your proving basket. Heavily sprinkle the tea towel with flour. Uncover your dough and sprinkle it with a little more flour. Using a scraper, scoop/scrape the dough into the lined basket, then sprinkle it with a little more flour and press down fairly firmly to smooth the top. This is the only shaping you will need for this loaf – easy peasy!

You can use a loaf tin to make this loaf, as follows: heavily dust your work surface with flour, then tip your dough on to it. Roll the dough in the flour, then place it in a 28cm x 12cm x 10cm loaf tin, sprinkle it with a little more flour and press down fairly firmly to smooth the top.

Leave to rise for 2 hours (the flour on the surface of the bread will start to crack when it's ready).

MAKES 1 LARGE LOAF

DAY 1: THE PRE-FERMENT

110g rye starter
(see page 33)

220g cold water

160g rye flour

DAY 2

200g cold water

12g fine sea salt

300g rye flour, plus
extra for dusting

YOU WILL NEED

a baking stone

a water spray

a baker's peel or
a wooden board

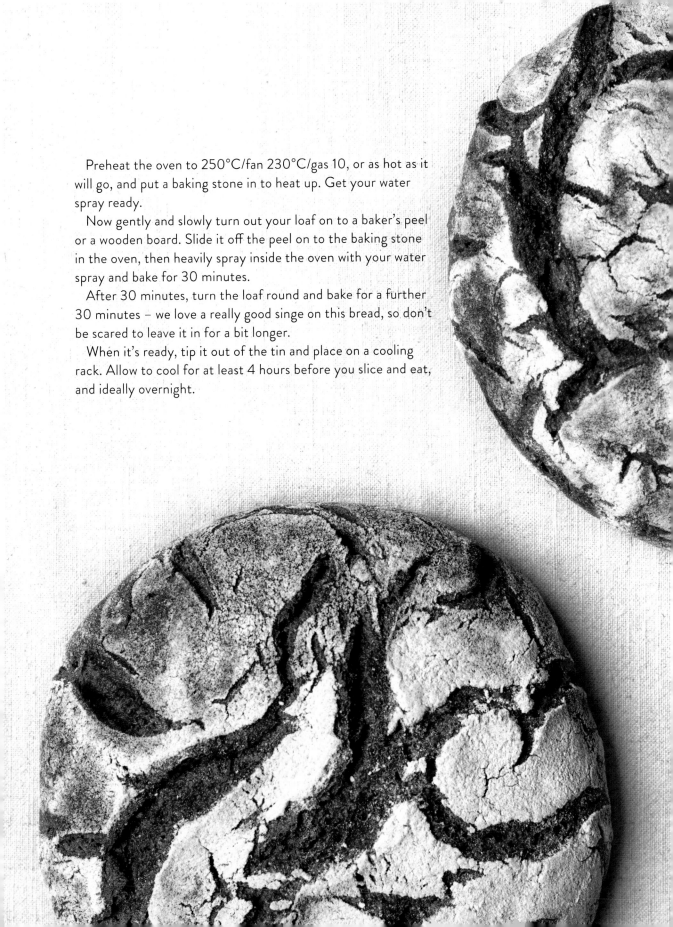

Preheat the oven to 250°C/fan 230°C/gas 10, or as hot as it will go, and put a baking stone in to heat up. Get your water spray ready.

Now gently and slowly turn out your loaf on to a baker's peel or a wooden board. Slide it off the peel on to the baking stone in the oven, then heavily spray inside the oven with your water spray and bake for 30 minutes.

After 30 minutes, turn the loaf round and bake for a further 30 minutes – we love a really good singe on this bread, so don't be scared to leave it in for a bit longer.

When it's ready, tip it out of the tin and place on a cooling rack. Allow to cool for at least 4 hours before you slice and eat, and ideally overnight.

PIZZA BASE SOUR

Who doesn't like pizza? Especially when it's sourdough pizza with its depth of flavour and its chewy crispy base with a hard high bake – now we want to see those blisters singed.

Feed your starter a good 8 hours before you make your sourdough pizza base.

Place the flour and water in a large bowl, then, with one hand, mix them together until combined. Cover and leave for 1 hour.

After an hour, add the starter, salt and olive oil, then, again with one hand shaped like a fork, gently bring together until just combined. Scrape the dough off your hand into the bowl, then take the dough out of the bowl and place it on a floured work surface, making sure you scrape all the dough out with a scraper to leave a clean bowl. Keep your bowl, as you will need it later.

Now, with your dough on the work surface and you 'poised like a puma' (see page 18), with the heel of your hand push the dough into the work surface and 'stretch and tear' for about 6 minutes, using the technique described on page 18. After 4 minutes, you will begin to feel the dough strengthen as the gluten develops.

Once your dough is fully developed, pour a little olive oil into the bowl you used earlier and put the dough back in, then give it a fold using the technique described on page 21. After folding, leave it to rest for an hour, then give the dough two more folds, resting for 30 minutes each time. Between folds you will need to cover the bowl with cling film, a tea towel or a shower cap. After the final fold, leave it in the bowl for an hour, then place in the fridge overnight.

Next morning, cut the dough into 200g pieces (or whatever size pizzas you would like), shape each one into a ball, and place on a floured surface. Sprinkle the dough with flour as well, then cover with an upside-down bowl and leave to rest for at least 1 hour, and ideally for about 2 hours.

MAKES 5

100g rye starter
(see page 33)

500g strong white
bread flour, plus extra
for dusting

400g water

7g fine sea salt

20g extra virgin olive oil

semolina or polenta,
for dusting

Mrs G's tomato sauce
(see opposite)

your desired toppings

YOU WILL NEED

a baking stone or an
upturned baking tray

a baker's peel or another
upturned baking tray

Preheat your oven to 250°C/fan 230°C/gas 10, or as hot as it will go, and put a baking stone or upturned baking tray in to heat up.

After resting, either roll or stretch the dough into a circle about 25cm in diameter. Place on an upturned tray or a baker's peel dusted with semolina or polenta. Spread your dough with the tomato sauce and load it with your desired toppings.

Slide the pizza on to the baking stone or upturned baking tray in the oven, and bake for 10 minutes, turning it round halfway through.

Remember to let it cool a little before eating.

MRS G'S TOMATO SAUCE /
MAKES ENOUGH FOR 4–5 PIZZA BASES

a splash of olive oil / 60g sliced onion (1 small onion) /
7 cloves of garlic, peeled and cut in half /
1 x 400g tin of chopped tomatoes / 1 level teaspoon fine sea salt

Put the olive oil into a pan on a medium heat and, when hot, add the onions and garlic. Cook for 5 minutes, stirring occasionally, until the onions are soft and just starting to caramelize.

Add the tinned tomatoes, bring to the boil, then simmer for 9 minutes, still stirring occasionally.

Blitz with a hand blender until smooth, then stir in the salt.

LAMMAS DAY

At Bread Ahead on 1 August we celebrate Lammas Day, a Christian festival to mark the year's first harvesting of the wheat.

For Southwark Cathedral, the arrival of Bread Ahead opposite their gates and the constant smell of baking led them to make the celebration of Lammas Day part of their keeping of the Christian year. As a Eucharistic community, bread is an essential element of worship – it is a staple of both altar and table.

Lammas Day comes from the old English 'hlaf masse', which translates as 'loaf mass'. Traditionally, in pre-Reformation times, Christians would take their first loaves of bread from the new wheat harvest to church to get them blessed as a celebration of transformation, rebirth and new beginnings. The practice has been revived in some places in more recent years.

Lammas Day is a day we come together as a community: Bread Ahead, Southwark Cathedral and Borough Market. We start with the delivery of the grain, which the Dean of Southwark blesses. He also helps us to mill the wheat into flour for our Lammas Day bread, which will be used in the service at the cathedral.

Then there is a procession from the cathedral to Bread Ahead, where the bishop blesses the bakery, the bakers, all the staff, the millers, the farmers, our bread, flour and grain. After that, in another procession, we head off to the cathedral with our first baked loaf, a wheatsheaf and several Cathedral loaves for the service.

THE PRESENTATION OF THE LAMMAS LOAF

Brothers and sisters in Christ, the people of God in ancient times presented to the Lord an offering of first-fruits as a sign of their dependence upon God for their daily bread.

At this Lammastide, we bring a newly baked loaf from newly harvested wheat, baked by BREAD AHEAD in thanksgiving to God for his faithfulness.

Jesus said, 'I am the bread of life; those who come to me shall never be hungry and those who believe in me shall never thirst.' (John 6.35)

The Lammas loaf is brought to the president, who says:

'Blessed are you, Lord God of all creation;
You bring forth bread from the fields
And give us the fruits of the earth in their seasons.
Accept this loaf, which we bring before you,
Made from the harvest of your goodness.
Let it be for us a sign of your fatherly care.
Blessed are you, Lord our God,
Worthy of our thanksgiving and praise.
Blessed be God for ever.'

THE WHEATSHEAF

We bake these for Lammas Day and make a few throughout the rest of the year for wholesale customers to use in displays. We make fairly large versions that certainly wouldn't fit in a domestic oven, so the recipe below is for a small one.

Put the flour and salt into a large bowl or mixer, then give a little stir to distribute the salt. In another bowl or a jug, dissolve the yeast in the water, then pour the mixture into the flour and salt. Mix together until all is incorporated and a dough is formed. Dust it with flour, then wrap the dough in cling film and put into the fridge for 2 hours.

When the 2 hours are up, take your dough out of the fridge and cut off a 300g piece. Shape it into a ball – this will form your base template. Wrap the rest of the dough in cling film and put it back into the fridge (only ever take out what you need at one time).

Preheat the oven to 140°C/fan 120°C/gas 1.

Roll out your 300g piece of dough on a lightly floured surface until it is about 40cm long. Then roll the top half of the dough widthways until it is 28cm wide, and the bottom half until it is 20cm wide.

At the bottom of your rolled-out dough, cut the edge straight. Mark out 18cm along the bottom of the dough, then from the middle of the base make a mark 11cm up. From that mark, measure 5cm on each side and mark these. From these marks, cut down to the bottom marks each side of the 18cm. Cut the dough above that into a circular shape. So you should have something that looks like a mushroom or a keyhole. You can make a paper pattern if you like (see the photo on page 63).

Place the dough shape on a baking tray lined with baking paper. Keep the trimmings, adding them to the rest of the dough in the fridge for later.

MAKES 1 SHEAF

1kg strong white bread flour, plus extra for dusting

2g fine sea salt

2g fresh yeast

500g water

2 currants, to decorate

1 egg, beaten, for the eggwash

Now make the stems. Take a piece of dough weighing about 3g and roll it out into a little sausage, starting from the middle and moving your hands outwards towards the ends, making a nice even strip. You need to make 40 of these, each 12cm long.

Place your first 2 stems on the outsides of the lower half of your mushroom-shaped template with their ends just over the edge at the bottom, then start to work your way in on both sides towards the middle, making sure the stems are placed tight up against each other. Cut the stems to fill any gaps. Once you have covered the base you need to hide the cut stems, so start to place more full stems on top of the cut stems, beginning from the middle – this will add a bit of height.

To make the rope, take 3 pieces of dough weighing about 20g each and roll them out into strips about 16cm long (they should be longer than the middle of your sheaf where the stems and corn meet). Press the 3 ends together and tightly plait them (see page 25).

Tuck one end of your plait under the edge of the top of the stems, then at the other end cut off any excess rope (do not throw this away) and tuck it in under the opposite side. Cut the excess rope into two pieces, tuck them under one side of the rope at an angle and fold over.

To make the corn ears, take some pieces of dough about 20g each and roll them into a sausage shape about 7cm long. Place them lengthways on your work surface, hold your scissors on the side about 1cm from the base, and with the tip of your scissors snip into the dough at an angle about 5mm deep and 2cm long. Repeat this 3 or 4 times along the length of the corn ear, then repeat along the opposite side and along the top. This should now resemble an ear of corn. You need to make 55 of these.

Place the first corn ears in the middle of the top of the mushroom shape, just over the edge so that none of the base is showing. When you get to the sides, start to place the ears more lengthways as you move down the sheaf. The last corn ear you place on the side should be touching the rope. Once you have done the outer ears, start the same procedure on the next layer, making sure the tops of the ears are overlapping the bottom of the first layer. Repeat until the sheaf is covered, and when you get to the last corn ear, make it a little bit longer (9cm) so that you can bend it over the rope.

For the field mouse, take a piece of dough weighing about 10g and roll it into a rounded teardrop shape. To make the ears, snip the dough twice, 2cm from the pointy end and about 1cm deep. With your finger and thumb, press the dough down in front of your cuts so your ears are more sticky-outy. Press 2 currants into the dough just in front of the ears to make the eyes. Take 1g of dough and roll it into a tail. Place the tail on the wheatsheaf stems and give it a curl, then place the mouse at the end of the tail.

To finish, take your scissors and tidy up any bits left showing round the base, then brush with the eggwash.

Pop your wheatsheaf into the oven and bake for 1 hour and 50 minutes. After an hour of baking, take the sheaf out of the oven and eggwash it again so it gets a lovely shine, and cover the stems with tin foil so they don't get too brown. Return the sheaf to the oven for another 50 minutes, then take out of the oven and leave to cool for a good few hours.

Your wheatsheaf will keep for a couple of weeks, and if varnished for a couple of months or longer.

You can also use this recipe to make name plaques and decorated breads for celebrations. We make them for some of our wholesale customers as a bread display.

ENGLISH BAKING

It's hard to think of English baking without thinking of the quintessential English tradition of afternoon tea: scones, buns, cream cakes and, of course, crustless finger sandwiches. We are known all around the world for the sandwich, famously created in the eighteenth century by the 4th Earl of Sandwich, a notorious gambler, who is said to have come up with the idea of putting his meal between two pieces of bread so that it could be eaten with one hand without having to leave the gambling table.

Most people think of English bread as being a thick slice of crusty white, like our handsome white tin loaf on page 69. In the 1960s, the development of the Chorleywood bread process meant that bread could be mechanically produced in a shorter amount of time using lower-protein wheat grain, and with all sorts of additives involved. This led to the cheap, tasteless, pappy white sliced and packaged bread that is everywhere today, and to the closure of many small family-run bakeries around the country.

But the bread revolution is here! And it starts with you, yes, YOU! Bake your own bread and make sure you support your local bakery. Remember, great bread takes time, love, and of course a little help from Bread Ahead.

THE HANDSOME WHITE TIN

This is Mrs G's favourite loaf – with its golden and blistered crust, it's perfect for all sandwiches and particularly ideal for a bacon sandwich. This blows away any of the pappy white bread that you find in supermarkets.

MAKES I MIGHTY TIN LOAF, OR 2 SMALLER LOAVES

470g strong white bread flour, plus extra for dusting

10g salt

340g water

1g fresh yeast

180g stiff starter (see page 33)

oil, for the bowl

YOU WILL NEED

a water spray

First weigh the flour and salt and mix them just enough for them to get to know each other. Put the water and yeast into a separate bowl and combine with one hand until the yeast is dissolved. Now add the starter to the water. You will need to combine this mixture as much as you can – a squeezing action with your hands really helps to break it all up.

Once you have combined it as best you can, add the water mixture to the flour and salt. Work it in (this takes about 1 minute), then scrape out your dough on to a floured work surface. Keep the bowl to one side, as you will need it later.

Now, with your dough on the work surface and you 'poised like a puma' (see page 18), with the heel of your hand push the dough into the work surface and 'stretch and tear', using the technique described on page 18, for about 8 minutes. After the first 5 minutes you will begin to feel the dough strengthen as the gluten develops.

Lightly oil the bowl you used earlier and put the dough back in. You now need to give it a fold, using the technique described on page 21. After folding, leave it to rest for 1 hour, then give the dough two more folds, resting for an hour each time. Between folds you will need to cover the bowl with cling film, a tea towel or a shower cap. After the final fold, leave it for a further 30 minutes.

Gently scrape out your dough from the bowl and place it on a lightly floured work surface. You can now carry on and make one mighty tin loaf, using a bread tin 28cm x 12cm x 10cm, or divide it in half to make 2 loaves, using two bread tins 20cm x 10cm x 6cm, or turn one of the halves into a lardy cake (see page 78). Shape into a ball or balls (see page 22) and place on a floured surface, then cover with a tea towel and leave to rest for 10 minutes.

Now shape the dough (see page 22). Once shaped, place seam side down in your oiled tin or tins, cover with cling film or a shower cap, and leave to prove until risen up round the top.

You can bake the bread now, but for the best result, lightly cover with a shower cap and place in the fridge for about 10–12 hours, or overnight, and bake the following day.

When you are ready to bake, preheat your oven to 240°C/fan 220°C/gas 9. Get your water spray ready.

Take your loaves out of the fridge and uncover, then pop them into the preheated oven. With your water spray on fine mist, spray lightly inside the oven. Bake for about 25 minutes, then turn the tins round and bake for a further 15 minutes if making one large loaf. If making two smaller loaves, bake for 25 minutes, then turn and bake for a further 5 minutes. Now take out of the oven and remove from the tin or tins. The bread should be golden all over, with a golden blistered top. If it is still pale on the sides, put back into the tin or tins and return to the oven for another few minutes.

Leave to cool, then enjoy your beautiful bread!

MANCHETS

Manchets are little enriched buns dating from medieval times, made with the highest grade of flour and often flavoured with things like rose, nutmeg and cinnamon. References to manchets date back to 1526, during Henry VIII's reign, when a menu for the medieval aristocracy included mention of 'manchettes'.

This is our take on these small medieval buns, which are a real delight either sweet or savoury. They can be served on their own, or with butter and jam, or with cold meats and pickles.

MAKES 12

148g strong white bread flour, plus extra for dusting

90g wholemeal flour

18g caster sugar

6g fine sea salt

160g milk

5g fresh yeast

22g rye starter (see page 33)

5g honey

45g unsalted butter

1 egg, beaten, for the eggwash

optional toppings: caraway seeds, sugar nibs, caster sugar, fennel seeds, mustard seeds

First line a 40cm x 30cm baking tray with baking paper.

Measure the flours, sugar and salt into a bowl and combine, just enough for them to get to know each other. Make a well in the centre.

Put the milk into another bowl, then add the yeast, starter and honey and mix until dissolved. Pour the liquid into the well in the centre of the flour.

With one hand shaped like a fork, gently bring together until just combined – it will only take a minute or two. Scrape the dough off your hand into the bowl, then take the dough out of the bowl and place it on a floured work surface, making sure you scrape all the dough out with a scraper to leave a clean bowl.

Now, with your dough on the work surface and you 'poised like a puma' (see page 18), with the heel of your hand push the dough into the work surface and 'stretch and tear', using the technique described on page 18, for about 6 minutes. Form the dough into a ball, sprinkle with a little flour, then cover with a tea towel and leave to rest for 10 minutes.

Uncover the dough and begin to work in the butter, adding it a little at a time, and using the 'stretch and tear' technique to combine. Continue until all the butter is incorporated, being careful not to add it too quickly, as the dough will become greasy. Once all the butter is incorporated, continue to 'stretch and tear' for a further minute, then cover the dough with a tea towel and leave on your work surface for 10 minutes.

Divide the dough into 40g pieces and roll them into tight little balls (see page 25). Place them on the prepared baking tray, leaving some space between them as you don't want them 'kissing'. Loosely cover with cling film or a tea towel and leave them until they have just about doubled in size (about 2–3 hours).

Preheat your oven to 200°C/fan 180°C/gas 6. Gently uncover the plump buns and brush them with the eggwash, then sprinkle with your chosen toppings. For savoury buns, try caraway seeds, fennel seeds and leave a few plain. For sweet ones, try some with sugar nibs and some with caster sugar.

Bake the buns for 8 minutes, then turn the tray round and bake them for a further 2 minutes, until golden brown. Check that the bases are lightly golden too before removing them from the oven.

Once out of the oven, place the buns on a cooling rack. While they are still warm, fill the savoury buns with cold meats or a generous piece of cheese, and the sweet ones with butter and jam. Then indulge in a sixteenth-century baking tradition.

SCONES

The humble scone is a real symbol of English baking and brings any afternoon tea to life.

500g plain flour, plus extra for dusting

2 teaspoons bicarbonate of soda

2 teaspoons cream of tartar

2 teaspoons caster sugar

2 teaspoons fine sea salt

80g cold unsalted butter, diced small

250g buttermilk

90g full fat milk

1 egg, beaten, for the eggwash

YOU WILL NEED

a 6cm fluted pastry cutter

Preheat your oven to 200°C/fan 180°C/gas 6 and line a baking tray with baking paper.

Sift the flour, bicarbonate of soda, cream of tartar, sugar and salt into a large bowl, and mix together just enough for them to get to know each other. Add the cold diced butter and rub together with your fingertips until the butter is incorporated into the flour. It should look like fine sand.

Add the buttermilk and milk, mix together until the dough begins to take shape, then take the dough out of the bowl and pop it on to your work surface, making sure you scrape it all out. Bring the dough together by kneading with your hands, being careful not to overmix – once it is all together and happy you need to stop, cover and leave to rest for 5 minutes.

On a lightly floured work surface, roll out the dough to a thickness of 2cm and cut out the scones using a 6cm fluted pastry cutter. Layer the trimmings on top of each other, re-roll and cut again. Place the scones on the prepared baking tray and brush with the eggwash. Bake for 8 minutes, then turn the tray round and bake for a further 2 minutes, until golden brown. Remove from the oven and place on a cooling rack.

Serve warm, with extra-thick Jersey cream and jam.

WILD GARLIC + CHEDDAR SCONES / MAKES 24

I (Matt) made these beauties to celebrate the season of wild garlic for St George's at Borough Market, and they flew off the stall hot from the oven. If wild garlic is not in season, you can use spring onions and herbs instead.

500g plain flour, plus extra for dusting / 2 teaspoons bicarbonate of soda / 2 teaspoons cream of tartar / 2 teaspoons caster sugar / 2 teaspoons fine sea salt / 80g cold unsalted butter / a dozen or so wild garlic leaves, roughly chopped / 200g mature Cheddar cheese, grated / 2 teaspoons English mustard powder / 250g buttermilk / 90g full fat milk / 1 egg, beaten, for the eggwash

Follow the method for plain scones on page 75, adding the chopped garlic leaves, grated cheese and mustard powder just before you add the buttermilk and milk. Stir to combine, then add the buttermilk and milk and follow the rest of the recipe as given.

ORANGE + RAISIN SCONES / MAKES 24

No need for jam and cream – these are stars in their own right, especially warm.

300g raisins / 2 oranges, zested and juiced / 500g plain flour, plus extra for dusting / 2 teaspoons bicarbonate of soda / 2 teaspoons cream of tartar / 2 teaspoons caster sugar / 2 teaspoons fine sea salt / 80g cold unsalted butter / 250g buttermilk / 90g full fat milk / 1 egg, beaten, for the eggwash

Put the raisins into a bowl and add the orange zest and juice. Leave to soak overnight.

Follow the plain scone recipe on page 75, adding the soaked raisins just before you add the buttermilk and milk. Stir in the raisins, add the juice they were soaking in, then the buttermilk and milk, and follow the rest of the recipe as given.

THE BREAD AHEAD PASTY

The pasty might be most strongly associated with Cornwall, but we are pretty proud of our own Bread Ahead version. We teach making and baking these pasties during our full-day English class, for the students to have for their lunch, and they never disappoint.

The clotted cream tip came from Mr Chapman, one of our bakery school teachers.

MAKES 8

SHORTCRUST PASTRY

500g strong white bread flour, plus extra for dusting

½ teaspoon fine sea salt

300g cold unsalted butter, diced

100g full fat milk

4 egg yolks, beaten

1 egg, beaten, for the eggwash

THE FILLING

350g Maris Piper potatoes, chopped into small dice

200g Cheddar cheese, grated

125g white onion, diced

½ tablespoon fine sea salt

several twists of black pepper

8 teaspoons clotted cream

Put the flour and salt into a large bowl, mix together just enough for them to get to know each other, then add the cold diced butter. Using your fingers, rub the butter into the flour until the mixture looks like fine breadcrumbs. Add the milk and the egg yolks, and continue mixing until you have a dough. Wrap it in cling film and put it into the fridge to rest for a couple of hours.

While the pastry is chilling, prepare your filling. Place the chopped potatoes, grated cheese and diced onion in a bowl. Season with the salt and pepper and give it all a quick stir.

Once the pastry is chilled, take it out of the fridge to soften so that you can roll it out.

Line a baking tray with baking paper. Roll out the pastry on a lightly floured surface to a thickness of 2mm and cut out 6 circles 15cm in diameter (a saucer works well as a guide). Roll out the trimmings and cut 2 more, then eggwash the outer rims of the circles and divide the filling equally between them, placing it in the middle of each circle. Dollop a teaspoon of clotted cream on top of each mound of filling.

Fold over the pastry to enclose the filling and crimp together to seal. Place on the prepared baking tray and chill in the fridge for 10–15 minutes.

Preheat your oven to 200°C/fan 180°C/gas 6.

Take the tray of pasties out of the fridge, brush them with the eggwash, and bake for 40 minutes, until piping hot and crispy golden brown.

THE LARDY CAKE

Lardy cake is also known as lardy bread or lardy Johns. It is sometimes made without currants, but is always spiced.

When we are teaching this recipe, a lot of people ask if they can substitute butter for the lard, but it's called lardy cake, so celebrate the lard. When the lard and sugar melt together, they form a delicious, sticky, caramelized crust, and that's what makes this cake so special.

Put the currants, both sugars, spices and lemon zest into a bowl and mix well.

After the white dough has had its prove, roll it out on a lightly floured surface into a 30cm x 15cm rectangle. With the shortest side in front of you, place small knobs of the lard all over the dough and cover with the currant and spice mix. Press the mixture into the dough, evenly over the lard, picking up any lost currants and popping them back in. Fold the top and bottom halves to meet in the middle, then fold this over so you have a sandwich. Cover the dough and rest for 30 minutes in the fridge, then repeat the rolling and folding and leave for another 30 minutes. Repeat the rolling and folding once more, then leave covered to rest for a final 30 minutes in the fridge.

Grease a 20cm x 10cm x 6cm loaf tin with lard. Give the dough a little roll, then pop it into your greased tin. Rub some more lard over the top and sprinkle heavily with demerara sugar. Loosely cover with a tea towel, then leave to prove until the dough looks puffed up and proud, and has come just above the top of the tin (this should take about 2 hours).

Preheat your oven to 180°C/fan 160°C/gas 4.

Put the tin on a baking tray, place in the oven and bake for 40 minutes. Always remember to put the tin on a tray, as the lard does bubble out.

Once baked, remove the cake from the tin straight away – but be careful, as there will be lots of hot melted fat in the tin. By removing the lardy cake straight away you can maintain the crispness on the outside and prevent sogginess.

Serve warm, with butter or cream and a mug of tea, and salute the LARD!

SERVES 6–8

150g currants

60g caster sugar

60g demerara sugar, plus extra for sprinkling

2 teaspoons ground mixed spice

½ teaspoon ground cinnamon

a pinch of ground ginger

zest of 1 lemon

½ a batch of white tin dough (see page 69), at the stage before it goes into the tin

plain flour, for dusting

100g lard, cut into small dice, plus extra for greasing

BATH BUNS

These buns were supposedly created in the eighteenth century by William Oliver, who later invented those lovely Bath Oliver biscuits as a less fattening alternative! Traditionally they used to have a lump of sugar placed in the middle before being baked. Bath buns are still popular in Bath today, and this is our version of them.

MAKES 12

all the ingredients for the Devonshire split recipe (see page 86)

plain flour, for dusting

1 egg

170g mixed dried fruit (30g chopped prunes, 40g mixed peel, 40g currants, 35g raisins and 25g sultanas)

80g sugar nibs

12 glacé cherries

THE SUGAR GLAZE
100g water

100g sugar

20g liquid glucose

YOU WILL NEED

a water spray

a kitchen thermometer

Follow the recipe for Devonshire splits (see page 86), until the end of the 1-hour prove.

Roll out the dough on a lightly floured surface to about 1cm thick. Now this might seem a bit strange, but you want to cut up the dough, so, using a dough scraper, chop your dough roughly all over, so it's all in little pieces (see picture), then add the egg and chop through again. Once the egg is mostly incorporated, sprinkle the fruit and half the sugar nibs over, and again chop through.

Divide the dough into 12 equal pieces and place them carefully on baking trays lined with baking paper, making sure you leave some space between them. Place a glacé cherry in the middle of each one, sprinkle with the rest of the sugar nibs, then cover with a tea towel and leave to rise for 1 hour.

Preheat your oven to 180°C/fan 160°C/gas 4. Get your water spray ready.

Place your buns in the oven and lightly spray inside the oven with your water spray. Bake for 14 minutes, until golden brown.

While your buns are baking, make the glaze. Measure the water, sugar and liquid glucose into a heavy-based saucepan and place on a low heat to dissolve the sugar and glucose. Turn up the heat to a rolling simmer, then continue to simmer until it reaches 103°C on a kitchen thermometer.

Once your beautiful buns are out of the oven, glaze them straight away, and enjoy them warm.

CHELSEA BUNS

Chelsea buns were originally made at the Old Chelsea Bun House, a shop in Chelsea frequented by royalty in the eighteenth century.

So, before we opened our new site in Chelsea, the three of us came up with our version of these buns and it has become a firm favourite at the Chelsea branch of the Bread Ahead bakery on Pavilion Street, with people buying hundreds every Saturday. If you time your visit right, you can pick them up warm from the bakery – or use the recipe below to make them at home.

Sift the flour into a large bowl, then add the salt and sugar and mix well. Put the milk, crumbled yeast, lemon zest and egg yolk into another bowl or jug and whisk to combine well and dissolve the yeast. Add the milk mixture to the dry ingredients, then, with one hand shaped like a fork, gently bring together until just combined into a dough.

Scrape the dough off your hand into the bowl, then tip the dough out of the bowl and place on a lightly floured work surface, making sure you scrape all the dough out with a scraper to leave a clean bowl. Keep the bowl to one side, as you will need it later.

Now, with your dough on the work surface and you 'poised like a puma' (see page 18), with the heel of your hand push the dough into the work surface and 'stretch and tear', using the technique described on page 18, for about 8 minutes. Shape the dough into a round, cover with a tea towel, and leave for 5 minutes.

Now add the softened butter. Break the butter into pieces of about 20g, then knead them in slowly one by one, not adding the next one until the previous one has been incorporated. Once the butter has been incorporated, shape your dough into a ball, pop it back into the bowl you used earlier, then cover with a shower cap and put it into the fridge overnight.

Next day, your dough should have pillowed up and will look proud and airy.

Melt the salted butter and put to one side.

MAKES 11 OR 12

500g strong white bread flour, plus extra for dusting

3g fine sea salt

10g caster sugar

280g full fat milk

10g fresh yeast

zest of 1 lemon

1 egg yolk

80g softened unsalted butter

THE FILLING

80g softened salted butter

120g soft light brown sugar

2 teaspoons ground mixed spice

1 teaspoon ground allspice

285g plump currants

Take your dough out of the bowl and again place on a lightly floured work surface. Using a rolling pin, roll it out to a 40cm x 35cm rectangle, making sure the longest side is nearest to you. Brush the melted butter over the rectangle of dough, leaving a small strip clear of any filling along the top edge, then brush this clear strip with a little water (this strip will be used to seal the dough once rolled). Evenly scatter the sugar, spices and currants for the filling over the butter.

Starting with the edge nearest to you, roll up the dough like a Swiss roll, gently pressing the filling-free edge into the dough to seal it. Try to roll it as tightly and neatly as possible. Wrap the roll in cling film, then pop it into the fridge for 20 minutes to firm up.

Line a 38cm x 26cm x 2cm baking tray with baking paper.

Take out the roll of dough and place it on a chopping board, then, with a sharp knife, slice it into 4cm slices. Arrange the slices on the prepared baking tray, evenly spaced out and not too close to each other or to the edges, then cover and leave to prove until the slices are touching each other (this should take a couple of hours).

Preheat your oven to 200°C/fan 180°C/gas 6.

Bake the buns for 12 minutes, then turn the tray round and bake them for a further 8 minutes, until golden, covering them with foil if the fruit starts to burn at any point.

While your buns are baking, make the glaze. Measure the water, sugar and liquid glucose into a heavy-based saucepan and place on a low heat to dissolve the sugar and glucose. Turn up the heat to a rolling simmer, then continue to simmer until it reaches 103°C on a kitchen thermometer. Take off the heat and leave to cool for 5 minutes, then stir in your cassis, if using.

Once your beautiful buns are out of the oven, paint them all over with the glaze, then sprinkle with a little crunchy demerara sugar and put them back into the oven for 2 more minutes.

Once they have cooled a little, pull them apart and serve still warm from the oven.

THE SUGAR GLAZE

200g water

200g sugar

40g liquid glucose

optional: 50g cassis

TO SPRINKLE

50g demerara sugar

YOU WILL NEED

a kitchen thermometer

DEVONSHIRE SPLITS

My (Louise's) mum would always tell me about when she was a young girl and they used to go to Combe Martin on holiday. The highlight was going to a little tea room and having Devonshire splits.

Generally forgotten and replaced by the scone, it's time to bring these babies back. These enriched little bread buns are the perfect addition to any afternoon tea, especially with a glass of bubbles!

Sift the flour, salt and sugar into a large bowl and mix together just enough for them to get to know each other. Put the milk, crumbled yeast and melted butter into a jug or bowl and whisk to combine and dissolve the yeast. Add the milk mixture to the dry ingredients and combine to form a dough.

Transfer to a lightly floured surface and knead by hand for 2 minutes, then roll into a ball, put back into a lightly floured bowl, cover and leave in a warm place for 1–1½ hours, until doubled in size.

Divide the dough into 12 equal pieces and roll each one into a nice smooth tight ball (see page 25). Place the balls on a lined baking tray, leaving some space between them, as they will spread. Sprinkle with flour and cover with a tea towel, then leave to prove for about 30 minutes until proud, puffed up and roughly doubled in size.

Preheat your oven to 200°C/fan 180°C/gas 6.

Once proved, place the splits in your preheated oven and bake for 15 minutes, until golden brown. Place on a rack and leave to cool.

To serve, split them with a knife (but not all the way through), fill them with extra thick cream and top with jam.

MAKES 12

450g plain flour, plus extra for dusting

½ teaspoon fine sea salt

1 teaspoon caster sugar

275g full fat milk

15g fresh yeast

50g unsalted butter, melted

cream and jam, to serve

TEA CAKES

These tea cakes are lightly spiced, yeasted and full of fruit. They were traditionally toasted in front of the fire. Not to be confused with the famous Tunnock's tea cakes, which are a marshmallow biscuit tea cake coated in chocolate.

Serve your tea cake toasted, with lots of salted butter and – of course – a mug of tea.

MAKES 15

225g plain flour

225g strong white bread flour, plus extra for dusting

40g soft dark brown sugar

2 eggs

200g full fat milk

20g black treacle

10g fine sea salt

25g fresh yeast

5g ground cinnamon

2g ground nutmeg

25g ground mixed spice

50g softened butter

100g sultanas

100g currants

100g raisins

100g mixed peel

zest of 1 orange

zest of 1 lemon

sunflower oil, for the bowl

1 egg, beaten, for the eggwash

Sift the flours into a large bowl. Add the sugar, eggs, milk, black treacle, salt and yeast, and with one hand shaped like a fork, gently bring together until just combined. Scrape the dough off your hand into the bowl, then take the dough out of the bowl and place on a lightly floured work surface, making sure you scrape all the dough out with a scraper to leave a clean bowl. Keep the bowl to one side, as you will need it later.

Now, with your dough on the work surface and you 'poised like a puma' (see page 18), with the heel of your hand push the dough into the work surface and 'stretch and tear', using the technique described on page 18, for about 6 minutes. Cover and leave for 5 minutes. Now add the spices and again 'stretch and tear' for a couple of minutes until incorporated evenly.

Next add the softened butter. Break the butter into small pieces, about 25g each, then 'stretch and tear' the pieces of butter in slowly one by one, not adding the next one until the previous one has been fully incorporated.

Lastly, mix all the dried fruit, peel and zest into the dough and 'stretch and tear' for 2–3 minutes, until incorporated evenly.

Rub a splash of sunflower oil over the inside of the bowl you used earlier, then shape the dough into a round and place it in the centre of the bowl.

You now need to fold the dough, using the technique described on page 21. After folding, leave it to rest for 30 minutes, then give the dough two more folds, resting for 30 minutes each time. Between folds you will need to cover the bowl with cling film, a tea towel or a shower cap. After the final fold, leave it for a further 30 minutes.

After that last rest, when your dough is swollen up with the folding and proving, scrape the dough out of the bowl back on to a floured work surface. Cut it into 85g pieces, 'pre-shape' these into balls (see page 25), and leave to rest for 15 minutes.

Shape each one into a tighter round, smooth ball and place on a 48cm x 32cm baking tray lined with baking paper, leaving plenty of space between them. Leave to prove until they have increased by half and are looking very proud and sexy, which should take about 1–1½ hours.

In the meantime, make the glaze. Put all the ingredients into a heavy-based saucepan and place on a low heat to slowly dissolve the sugar. Once it is dissolved, turn up the heat so you have a rolling simmer and bring up the temperature to 103°C on a kitchen thermometer. Take off the heat and strain the glaze.

Preheat your oven to 160°C/fan 140°C/gas 3.

Very gently brush your tea cakes all over with the eggwash, then pop them into the oven. Bake for 12 minutes, then turn up the oven to 180°C/fan 160°C/gas 4, turn the tray round, and bake for a further 2 minutes, after which time the tea cakes should be nice and golden and smelling beautiful.

Brush them liberally with the spiced sugar glaze and enjoy.

THE SPICED SUGAR GLAZE

4 strips of orange peel

3 strips of lemon peel

500g water

125g soft dark brown sugar

125g soft light brown sugar

50g liquid glucose

1 cinnamon stick, broken in half

10 whole cloves

6 whole star anise

12 allspice berries

1 tablespoon fennel seeds

a few sprigs of thyme or rosemary

YOU WILL NEED

a kitchen thermometer

CUSTARD TART

OK, ladies and gentlemen, this is pretty much the perfect custard tart, and Justin has had many marriage proposals as a result.

Make sure you bake the pastry enough, as no one likes a soggy bottom, and also be sure to take the tart out of the oven while it still has a lovely wobble to it, as the residual heat will finish the cooking process outside the oven.

SERVES 12

THE PASTRY

20g soft light
brown sugar

160g caster sugar

250g unsalted butter

4 egg yolks

450g strong white
bread flour, plus extra
for dusting

a pinch of fine sea salt

1 egg yolk, beaten, to seal

THE FILLING

1 vanilla pod

900ml double cream

9 egg yolks

100g caster sugar

1 whole nutmeg,
for grating

Place the light brown sugar, caster sugar and butter in a bowl and cream together until white and fluffy.

Add the egg yolks one at a time, incorporating them slowly to prevent curdling, then add the sifted flour and salt and mix until combined.

Roll the dough into a ball and flatten a little. Wrap in baking paper or cling film and place in the fridge for 5–6 hours, and ideally overnight.

Take the pastry out of the fridge and allow it to soften. Butter and flour a 30cm tart case, at least 3–4cm deep (you can also make smaller tarts in individual cases).

Preheat your oven to 180°C/fan 160°C/gas 4.

Roll your dough out on a floured surface to 3mm thickness and line your tart case with it, being sure to press it right into the edges. Chill once more in the fridge, for 2–3 hours this time, or 45 minutes in the freezer (though again ideally overnight).

Take the tart case straight from the fridge or freezer, cover it with cling film or baking paper, then fill with baking beans and bake for 18 minutes, or until the edges are golden brown. Remove the cling film or paper and beans and bake for a further 10–12 minutes, or until golden brown all over (do not under-bake the tart case, as no one likes a soggy bottom and you will miss out on the moment when your spoon goes through the tart and you get to the pastry and then crunch! Ooh!).

Remove the tart case from the oven and brush with the egg yolk (this is to seal any holes or cracks in the case). Still in its tin, place on a cooling rack and leave the pastry to cool completely. Turn the oven down to 120°C/fan 100°C/gas ½.

While your pastry is cooling, make the filling. Slit the vanilla pod lengthways and scrape out the seeds. Put the seeds and pod into a saucepan with the double cream and bring slowly to the boil, to infuse the cream with the vanilla.

In a large bowl, whisk the egg yolks and sugar together for just a minute. Pour the boiling cream over the mixture, whisking constantly to prevent curdling. Pass through a fine sieve. If there is lots of froth on top, just spoon it off and discard.

Pour the warm custard mix into the blind-baked tart case, then grate all the nutmeg on top (do not use ready-ground nutmeg). Place carefully in the oven without spilling any of it down the sides of the pastry case; if you do, you will end up with soggy pastry, which is a no-no for a custard tart.

Bake for about 20 minutes, then carefully turn the tart round and bake for a further 6–8 minutes, or until there is only a small wobble in the centre of the tart. Take out of the oven and place on a rack to cool. Leave in the tin until cooled completely.

Best eaten on the day it's made, and at its absolute best when eaten within 2 hours of baking. But also very nice cold for breakfast.

THE COTTAGE LOAF

This was originally popular with bakers because its height meant that it saved room in the oven. Today it is rarely found in bakeries, perhaps because it isn't so easy to slice for sandwiches, but we love a beautiful cottage loaf, as it's got a great crust-to-crumb ratio, and it's such a lovely shape.

Melt the butter and leave to one side to cool.

Put the flour and salt into a large bowl and combine with one hand just enough to let them get to know each other, then make a well in the centre. Put the yeast, melted butter and water into another bowl, mix until dissolved, then pour the liquid into the well in the flour.

With one hand shaped like a fork, gently bring together until just combined. Scrape the dough off your hand into the bowl, then take the dough out of the bowl and place on a lightly floured work surface, making sure you scrape all the dough out with a scraper to leave a clean bowl. Keep the bowl to one side, as you will need it later.

Now, with your dough on the work surface and you 'poised like a puma' (see page 18), with the heel of your hand push the dough into the work surface and 'stretch and tear', using the technique described on page 18, for about 6 minutes.

Put the dough back into the bowl you used earlier. You now need to fold the dough, using the technique described on page 21. After folding, leave it to rest for an hour, then give the dough two more folds, resting for an hour each time. Between folds you will need to cover the bowl with cling film, a tea towel or a shower cap.

After the final rest, divide the dough into 2 pieces, roughly 600g for the bottom and 240g for the top. Form these loosely into balls and set them aside to rest for 10 minutes.

Now roll the two balls into tighter, firm balls (see page 22). Place the larger one on a floured lined baking tray, pop a floured finger into the middle of the ball and just wiggle it down. Place the smaller ball on top and again press a floured finger right though the top to meet in the middle, sealing them together.

MAKES I MEDIUM LOAF, TO SERVE 4

30g unsalted butter

510g strong white bread flour, plus extra for dusting

12g fine sea salt

3g fresh yeast

285g water

YOU WILL NEED

a water spray

Make 12 downward cuts round the bottom and 10 round the top (see picture), then cover and leave to prove for 45 minutes.

Preheat the oven to 240°C/fan 220°C/gas 9. Get your water spray ready.

Uncover the loaf and pop it into the preheated oven. With your water spray on fine mist, spray lightly inside the oven. Bake for about 30 minutes, then turn the tray round and bake for a further 10 minutes.

Once baked, place on a cooling rack. Delicious just with butter, or perfect as part of a ploughman's lunch.

TOASTED WHOLE WHEAT LOAF

This superb loaf always takes me (Matt) back to childhood and the first experience I had of home baking . . . all those years ago when wholemeal bread was something very few people even knew about.

Preheat the oven to 180°C/fan 160°C/gas 4. Pour the wholemeal grain on to a baking tray and toast in the oven for 10 minutes, until golden brown, then pop the toasted grain into a metal bowl and pour over 150g of water. Cover and leave overnight.

Next day, strain the grain, keeping the water to one side. Add enough water to the soaking water to make it up to 400g.

Place the flour, strained grain and salt in a large bowl and combine with one hand just enough to let them get to know each other, then make a well in the centre of the flour. Put the yeast and rye starter into another bowl with the 400g of water and grain water, mix until dissolved, then pour the liquid into the well in the flour.

With one hand shaped like a fork, gently bring together until just combined. Scrape the dough off your hand into the bowl, then take out the dough and place on a work surface, making sure you scrape all the dough out with a scraper to leave a clean bowl. Keep the bowl to one side, as you will need it later.

Now, with your dough on the work surface and you 'poised like a puma' (see page 18), with the heel of your hand push the dough into the work surface and 'stretch and tear', using the technique described on page 18, for about 6 minutes. Form loosely into a ball and pop back into the lightly oiled bowl you used earlier.

You now need to fold the dough, using the technique described on page 21. After folding, leave to rest for an hour, then give the dough two more folds, resting for an hour each time. Between folds you will need to cover the bowl with cling film, a tea towel or a shower cap.

MAKES 2 TIN LOAVES

150g wholemeal grain

515g wholemeal flour

12g salt

1g fresh yeast

100g rye starter
(see page 33)

400g water, including the grain soaking water

oil, for the bowl

YOU WILL NEED

a water spray

After the final rest, divide the dough into 2 equal pieces and shape them into batons. Once shaped, pop them seam side down into two oiled 20cm x 10cm x 6cm tins. Cover and leave to prove until the dough rises up around the top of the tins, which will take about 2–3 hours.

Preheat the oven to 240°C/fan 220°C/gas 9. Get your water spray ready.

Uncover the dough and put it into the preheated oven. With your water spray on fine mist, spray lightly inside the oven. Bake for about 30 minutes, then turn the tins round and bake for a further 10 minutes. Take them out and remove the loaves from the tins, then put them back into the oven, directly on the oven shelf, and bake for an extra 5 minutes. They should be golden all over – if not, put them back for another few minutes.

Place on a cooling rack, and enjoy.

MARRIAGE'S
THE MASTER MILLERS

FINEST
BREAD
FLOUR

Milled by

W & H MARRIAGE & SONS LTD
CHELMER MILLS, CHELMSFORD
01245 354455

Independent Flour Millers Since 1824

Visit our Website www.flour.co.uk

POTATO BREAD

This is one of the first breads Louise made at home with her grandmother, and we still bake it regularly at the bakery.

The potato adds a really nice soft crumb to this loaf. The beer gives it a lovely yeasty flavour, but it's also good made with water. Great for fried bread, as part of the English breakfast, but also bloody amazing made into eggy bread.

MAKES I LARGE LOAF

425g strong white bread flour, plus extra for dusting

200g mashed potato (made with about 300g potatoes such as King Edwards)

12g salt

2g fresh yeast

325g beer or water

semolina, for dusting

YOU WILL NEED

a baking stone or an upturned baking tray

a water spray

optional: a baker's peel or a wooden board

Place the flour, mashed potato and salt in a large bowl and combine with one hand just enough to let them get to know each other, then make a well in the centre. Put the yeast into another bowl with the beer or water, mix until dissolved, then pour the liquid into the well in the flour mixture.

With one hand shaped like a fork, gently bring together until just combined. Scrape the dough off your hand into the bowl, then take out the dough and place on a work surface, making sure you scrape all the dough out with a scraper to leave a clean bowl. Keep the bowl to one side, as you will need it later.

Now, with your dough on the work surface and you 'poised like a puma' (see page 18), mix together for about 6 minutes, making sure you scrape your dough to the centre throughout the mixing to make sure it develops evenly. It will still be sticky and wet after 6 minutes, but round it up into a ball, sprinkle with some flour and cover with a tea towel. Leave it to rest for 10 minutes. Meanwhile, line a proving basket with a tea towel and sprinkle it heavily with a mixture of flour and semolina.

Uncover the dough and reshape it into a ball. Pop it into the basket, seam side up, and sprinkle with more flour and semolina. Cover with a tea towel and leave to prove in the basket for about 4–6 hours.

Preheat the oven to 240°C/fan 220°C/gas 9, and put in a baking stone or upturned baking tray to heat up. Get your water spray ready.

Very gently turn your dough straight on to the baking stone or tray in the oven, or put it on to a baker's peel or a wooden board and slide it on to the stone or tray. With your water spray on fine mist, spray lightly inside the oven and bake for 35–40 minutes, until crispy dark.

Once baked, place on a rack to cool.

MUFFINS

Oh, do you know the muffin man / The muffin man, the muffin man /
Oh, do you know the muffin man / That lives on Drury Lane? /
Oh, yes, I know the muffin man / The muffin man, the muffin man /
Oh, yes, I know the muffin man / That lives on Drury Lane.

Pour the milk into a jug and whisk in the yeast until dissolved.
Whisk in the sugar and leave to stand for 10 minutes.

Put the flour, salt and butter into a large bowl and rub
together with your fingertips until you have fine crumbs. Stir in
the milk mixture until combined, then transfer to a lightly
floured surface and knead briefly until a smooth dough is
formed. This should take only 3 minutes, as you don't want to
overwork the dough.

Put the dough back into the bowl, cover, and leave
somewhere warmish to prove for 30 minutes.

Line a 24cm x 34cm baking tray with baking paper. On a
lightly floured surface, roll out the dough to 2cm thick. Then,
using a 7cm round pastry cutter, cut out 6–8 rounds and roll
out the trimmings to get a couple more. Place them on the
prepared tray, cover and leave for about 45 minutes to 1 hour,
until doubled in size. If you have some rings 7cm across and
6cm high, just butter the inside and dust with either semolina
or polenta, pop them on to the lined baking tray, then drop in
your 7cm cut pieces of dough and leave to prove in the rings
– this is what we use at Bread Ahead and it will give you a lovely
high muffin.

Preheat the oven to 180°C/fan 160°C/gas 4. Bake the
muffins for 5 minutes, then turn them over and bake for a
further 5 minutes, until lightly golden brown. Place on a rack
and leave to cool.

To serve, cut the muffins open and toast them. Serve warm,
with lashings of butter, or use them to make that classic, eggs
Benedict (don't forget a cheeky bloody Mary!).

MAKES 9 OR 10

225g full fat milk

20g fresh yeast

1 teaspoon caster sugar

450g plain flour, plus
extra for dusting

1 teaspoon fine sea salt

75g cold butter, diced

semolina, for dusting

YOU WILL NEED

a 7cm round pastry
cutter

optional: rings 7cm
across and 6cm high

ITALIAN BAKING

talian breads and baking differ not just from region to region, but from town to town, and even from Nonna to Nonna.

In Italy, you rarely sit down to supper without a baked loaf of bread in the centre of the table. Bread forms part of the meal but it can also be the meal itself, in dishes such as pizza, focaccia and bruschetta, and in salads like panzanella and soups and stews like ribollita.

We (Louise and Justin) still remember going to Naples and having our first Italian pizza – it really blew us away. Made with just a whisper of tomato sauce, some juicy thick mozzarella and a leaf of basil, it was simply done but tasted amazing. Italian baking is all about simplicity, which allows the quality of the ingredients to shine through.

We know that the Italians are all about love and passion (with a little football thrown in), and they carry that love and passion into their cooking, which really comes across in their methods of making and baking their breads, as you will learn throughout this chapter. With this in mind, we have tried to respect the simple but delicious ideas of Italian baking.

CIABATTA

Ciabatta might seem like it's been around for ever, but in fact it was created in 1982 by a baker in Verona as a home-grown alternative to the French baguette, which was gaining popularity in Italy. The ciabatta was brought to our shores a few years later by good old Marks & Spencer, and has been one of Italy's most popular exports ever since.

This slipper-shaped bread ('ciabatta' means 'slipper' in Italian) is both crispy and chewy, with a lovely open texture. It's a joy to make and an even bigger joy to eat. Just remember that this is a very wet and sticky dough – don't be tempted to add more flour, as it will change the whole dynamics of this beautiful bread.

Place your flour and salt in a large bowl and combine with one hand just enough to let them get to know each other, then make a well in the centre of the flour. Put the yeast and water into another bowl, mix until dissolved, then pour this liquid into the well in the flour.

With one hand bring the flour and liquid together to form a loose dough – it will be very sticky and wet, but don't worry. Scrape the dough off your hand back into the bowl, then tip the loose, sticky dough on to a work surface, making sure you scrape all the dough out with a scraper to leave a clean bowl. Keep the bowl to one side, as you will need it later.

Now, with your dough on the work surface, it's time for a bit of 'slapping the dough', using the technique described on page 21. You will need to repeat this for about 8 minutes (a nice little workout for those bingo wings!), bringing the dough together in the centre with your scraper to ensure that it develops evenly. After 3–4 minutes, you will begin to feel the dough becoming springier as the gluten develops, and after 8 minutes it will hold itself together and come away from the work surface.

Rub the inside of the bowl you used earlier with the olive oil, then place your dough in the centre. You now need to fold the dough, using the technique described on page 21. After folding, leave it to rest for 30 minutes (you might need a rest as well), then give the dough three more folds, resting it for 30 minutes each time. Between folds you will need to cover the bowl with cling film, a tea towel or a shower cap. After the

MAKES I LARGE PAIR OF SLIPPERS (EACH 40CM LONG), OR 2 PAIRS OF SMALLER SLIPPERS (EACH 20CM LONG)

400g strong white bread flour, plus extra for dusting

8g fine sea salt

6g fresh yeast

350g water

20g extra virgin olive oil

semolina, for dusting

YOU WILL NEED

a water spray

final fold, leave it for 30 minutes, then put it into the fridge for 10 minutes – the fridge time just firms up the dough ready for shaping.

Preheat your oven to 250°C/fan 230°C/gas 10, or as hot as it will go. Line a baking tray approximately 45cm x 38cm with baking paper, and sprinkle it with semolina. Get your water spray ready.

Remove your dough from the fridge and heavily flour both the top of the dough and your work surface, then gently work your scraper round the sides of the bowl to ensure the dough isn't sticking. Turn the bowl upside down to release the dough on to your floured work surface, then sprinkle the top of the dough with more flour.

Cut your dough into two slipper shapes. Don't worry if they're not perfect – you don't want to handle them too much, as you want to keep as much air in as possible for that light, airy texture when the bread is baked.

Turn your shapes over on to the floured surface, then lightly stretch them on to the lined baking tray. They should be about 40cm long and 8cm wide (or you can make 4 smaller ones 20cm long and 8cm wide). Cover with a cloth and leave to rest for 15 minutes.

With your water spray on fine mist, spray lightly inside the oven before putting in your ciabatta. Bake for 16 minutes – you want a good hard bake, as the ciabatta will collapse without the structure of proper crust, because it is so-o-o-o airy inside. Don't be afraid of the colour – the flavour is so much better and we love a bit of singe! Once the ciabatta is out of the oven, place it on a cooling rack.

These slippers make great sandwiches and garlic bread, or you can just serve them plain, with olive oil.

FOCACCIA

This Italian olive oil bread makes a really lovely centrepiece to any family feast. It can be thick or thin, decorated simply with just olive oil and herbs, or loaded with seasonal produce like tomatoes, red onion and olives.

Always remember to pop those dimples in, to make delicious olive oil pools on top of your focaccia.

Place your flour and salt in a large bowl and combine with one hand just enough to let the flour get to know the salt, then make a well in the centre of the flour. Put the water and yeast into another bowl, mix until dissolved, then pour the liquid into the well in the flour.

With one hand shaped like a fork, gently bring the mixture together until just combined. Scrape the dough off your hand back into the bowl, then take the dough out and place on a work surface, making sure you scrape all the dough out with a scraper to leave a clean bowl. Keep the bowl to one side, as you will need it later.

Now, with your dough on the work surface and you 'poised like a puma' (see page 18), with the heel of your hand push the dough into the work surface and 'stretch and tear', using the technique described on page 18, for about 8 minutes. After the first 4 minutes you will begin to feel a change in the dough as the gluten develops.

Pour 40g of the olive oil into the bottom of the bowl you used earlier and place the dough in the centre. Spread the oil from the bowl over the top of the dough and give the dough a fold, using the technique described on page 21 (this will also help incorporate the oil). After folding, leave to rest for 30 minutes (you might need a rest as well), then give the dough three more folds, resting for 30 minutes each time. Between folds you will need to cover the bowl with cling film, a tea towel or a shower cap. After the final fold, leave for 30 minutes, then move it to the fridge for 10 minutes – the fridge time just firms up the dough ready for shaping.

Preheat your oven to 220°C/fan 200°C/gas 7 and lightly oil a deep 30cm x 20cm baking tray.

MAKES 1 LARGE
FOCACCIA, ENOUGH
FOR 4–6 PEOPLE

500g strong white bread flour

10g sea salt

400g water

6g fresh yeast

80g extra virgin olive oil, plus extra for the top

TOPPINGS

fresh herbs, such as thyme, marjoram and rosemary

crunchy coarse sea salt

your choice of extra toppings, such as cherry tomatoes, red onions, sliced potatoes and olives

Take your dough out of the fridge and gently slide it on to the baking tray, then fold it in half lengthways and massage the rest of the oil over the surface of the dough, making sure it is evenly covered. With your fingertips, gently dimple the top of the dough to spread it out in the tray, making sure you cover the whole surface with indentations. This will trap little pools of oil and give your focaccia its traditional appearance.

Now for the toppings. We love it just with herbs such as thyme, marjoram and rosemary, plus olive oil and crunchy coarse sea salt, but don't be scared to add cherry tomatoes, sliced red onions, olives or some finely sliced new potatoes. Top the focaccia however you choose (but don't add the salt just yet), then lightly press the toppings down with your fingertips.

Leave for another 30 minutes to prove, until airy and beautifully proud, but don't cover it – the olive oil will act as a cover and stop the focaccia drying out. If you need to, you can now keep the finished focaccia in the fridge for up to 4 hours before baking. When you're ready, sprinkle it with crunchy coarse sea salt and bake in your preheated oven for 15 minutes, until crispy and golden brown.

Take out of the oven, place on a cooling rack and sprinkle with more extra virgin olive oil to fill up those dimples, so you have pools of fragrant oil on top. Place your focaccia in the middle of your table and tear to serve.

PAN PUGLIESE

This rustic Italian bread comes from the region of Puglia. It uses a mix of durum wheat and high-protein flour, which gives the bread a distinctive look, colour, flavour and crust. It's delicious served with any Italian food and perfect for making bruschetta topped with big flavours. You can also use the dough to make lovely rolls.

The night before you want to make your bread, make your biga. Dissolve the yeast in the water, then put into a bowl with the flour and combine fully. Cover and place in the fridge for 8–10 hours.

When you are ready to start making your dough (day 2), mix the flours and salt together in a bowl, then add the biga. Mix the yeast with the water and dissolve. Add to the flour and bring together to form a loose dough. Take out of the bowl and place on a work surface.

Now, with your dough on the work surface and you 'poised like a puma' (see page 18), with the heel of your hand push the dough into the work surface and 'stretch and tear', using the technique described on page 18, for about 4 minutes, then with your scraper bring the dough back together. It will be fully combined and starting to feel a little more elastic. Place in a lightly oiled bowl and cover, then leave to rest for 30 minutes.

Take your dough out of the bowl and give it a fold, using the technique described on page 21 (this will also help incorporate the oil into the dough). After folding, leave it to rest for 30 minutes (you might need a rest as well), then give the dough three more folds, resting for 30 minutes each time. Between folds you will need to cover the bowl with cling film, a tea towel or a shower cap. After the final fold, leave for another 30 minutes. While it is resting, line a proving basket or a bowl with a tea towel and dust it with a mixture of flour and semolina.

Gently take the dough out of the bowl. Shape it into a good round (see page 22), then place seam side up in the proving basket and dust with semolina. If making rolls, cut the dough into 12 equal pieces and roll them into nice smooth tight balls (see page 25). Roll them in semolina and place them on a baking tray lined with baking paper and sprinkled with more semolina, remembering to leave space between them. You may

MAKES I GORGEOUS
GOLDEN LOAF OR
12 CRACKING ROLLS

DAY I: THE BIGA
(SEE PAGE 14)

1g fresh yeast

60g water

100g strong white
bread flour

DAY 2

200g strong white
bread flour, plus extra
for dusting

200g durum wheat
or semolina

8g sea salt

4g fresh yeast

350g water

olive oil, for the bowl

semolina, for dusting

YOU WILL NEED

a Dutch oven (cast-iron
casserole)

a water spray

need to use two baking trays. Lightly cover with cling film and leave the dough to prove for about 30 more minutes, until risen to the top of the basket.

Preheat the oven to 250°C/fan 230°C/gas 10, or as hot as it will go, and put a Dutch oven (cast-iron casserole) in to heat up.

Carefully take your Dutch oven out of the oven. Gently turn the loaf out of the basket and place in the Dutch oven. Pop the lid on and bake for 30 minutes, then take off the lid and bake for a further 10 minutes, to get a nice golden crust on top. If you are making rolls, put the baking tray into the oven, spray the inside of the oven with your water spray, and bake for about 15 minutes, until golden brown with a little singe.

Take the bread out of the oven and place on a cooling rack. Once cool, enjoy this truly wonderful loaf. Take it on a picnic with cold meats and a hunk of cheese, not forgetting a nice bottle of vino rosso.

PIZZA

At Bread Ahead we believe that the secret of great pizza is all in the base, with a hard bake and a great crispy crunch. This simple two-day recipe will give your pizza a depth of flavour that will transport you to the streets of Naples, shouting, 'Bella, bella!'

You will start off using a rolling pin or just stretching out the base, but before you know it you will be throwing the dough in the air just like those classic Italian bakers in Naples.

The night before you want to make your pizza, make your poolish. Dissolve the yeast in the water, then add to the flour in a bowl and combine fully. Cover and place in the fridge for 8–10 hours.

Next day, put your flour and salt into a large bowl and combine with one hand just to let the flour get to know the salt. Now uncover your poolish (it will be nice and bubbly) and add it to the flour.

Mix the yeast with the water and add to the bowl.

With one hand shaped like a fork, gently bring the dough together until just combined. Scrape the dough off your hand back into the bowl, then take the dough out of the bowl and place on a lightly floured work surface, making sure you scrape all the dough out with a scraper to leave a clean bowl.

Now, with your dough on the work surface and you 'poised like a puma' (see page 18), with the heel of your hand push the dough into the work surface and 'stretch and tear', using the technique described on page 18, for about 6 minutes. After 4 minutes, you will begin to feel the dough strengthen as the gluten develops. Once your dough is fully developed, cut it into 2 equal pieces. Shape each piece into a ball and place on a floured surface, then cover with a tea towel and leave to rest for 1 hour.

Preheat the oven to 250°C/fan 230°C/gas 10, or as hot as it will go, and put a baking stone or an upturned baking tray in to heat up. The baking stone will give you a faster and more authentic bake for your pizza.

Uncover your dough, which should have doubled in size by now. Roll it or stretch it into a circle about 25cm in diameter.

MAKES 2 REGULAR PIZZA
BASES, OR, IF YOU HAVE
A GREAT BIG OVEN,
ONE BICYCLE-WHEEL
SIZE PIZZA

DAY 1: THE POOLISH
(SEE PAGE 15)

2g fresh yeast

50g water

50g strong white
bread flour

DAY 2

250g strong white
bread flour, plus extra
for dusting

4g fine sea salt

4g fresh yeast

175g water

semolina, for dusting

Mrs G's tomato sauce
(see page 55)

your desired toppings

YOU WILL NEED

a baking stone or an
upturned baking tray

a baker's peel or a
wooden board

Place it on a baker's peel or wooden board dusted with semolina
or polenta. Spread your dough with the tomato sauce and load
it with your desired toppings, then slide it on to the baking
stone or upturned baking tray in the oven and bake for 8–10
minutes, turning it round once halfway through baking.

Take your pizza out of the oven and enjoy a taste sensation,
but remember to let it cool a little before getting stuck in,
otherwise there will be burnt mouths all round, and we all know
how that feels.

BREAD
AHEAD
BAKERY & SCHOOL

CHEESE &
OLIVE STICK
£2.50 | £4.00 for 2

with Moroccan Green
Olives & Red Leicester

CHEESE AND OLIVE STICKS

These have been a great success on the Bread Ahead bakery stall at Borough Market. The bakery is 2 seconds from the stall, so we bake them fresh, then run to the stall with them and sell them hot! If you hear the guys calling out, 'Hot cheese and olive sticks on the stall now!' when you are walking through Borough Market, head over quickly before they sell out.

These will hold their shaped, unbaked form in the fridge for a good 12 hours, so you can bake them when you need to – but make sure you serve them deliciously warm!

MAKES 8 LARGE STICKS

700g strong white bread flour, plus extra for dusting

14g fine sea salt

6g fresh yeast

475g water

200g cheese, cut into 2cm cubes (we use half red Leicester and half Cheddar, but you can use whatever cheese you like)

220g pitted green olives (you can use black olives, or do half and half)

100g polenta

optional: 100g sliced red onions and/or a couple of chopped chillies

100g polenta

Begin your dough the day before you want to bake the sticks. Put the flour and salt into a large bowl and combine with one hand just enough to let the flour get to know the salt, then make a well in the centre of the flour. Put the yeast and water into another bowl, mix until dissolved, then pour the liquid into the well in the flour.

With one hand shaped like a fork, gently bring together until just combined. Scrape the dough off your hand back into the bowl, then take out the dough and place on a lightly floured work surface, making sure you scrape all the dough out with a scraper to leave a clean bowl. Keep the bowl to one side, as you will need it later.

Now, with your dough on the work surface and you 'poised like a puma' (see page 18), with the heel of your hand push the dough into the work surface and 'stretch and tear', using the technique described on page 18, for about 8 minutes. When your dough feels elastic and strong, cover and leave for 8 minutes to relax the dough (and your arm).

Now you need to work in the cheese and olives, and, if you're feeling cheeky, a few sliced red onions and a couple of chopped chillies as well. Gradually add the cheese and olives to the dough, and again 'stretch and tear' until everything is incorporated. Try not to break down the cheese too much – large chunks will melt better in the oven. Once incorporated, put the dough into the bowl you used earlier, cover with cling film, a tea towel or a shower cap, and pop into the fridge for between 16 and 24 hours.

115 ITALIAN BAKING

Next day, line a couple of baking trays with baking paper. Take the dough out of the fridge and leave for 1 hour, then cut it into 200g pieces. Sprinkle all the polenta over the pieces of dough and roll them into long sticks (see page 25) about 30cm long, making sure each is well coated in polenta – it will add a lovely tasty crunch to the bread. If you are having difficulty rolling the sticks out, just roll them to 15cm and leave them to rest for a couple of minutes, then roll out again. The dough will be relaxed and easier to roll. If you have any leftover polenta, just brush it into a bowl and re-use next time, or use it for dusting baking trays.

Place the sticks on the prepared baking trays and pop them into the fridge for at least a couple of hours. When you are ready to bake, preheat the oven to 220°C/fan 200°C/gas 7.

Bake for about 16 minutes, until golden brown and piping hot. The cheese should be oozing out of the golden-brown sticks – if not, give them another minute or two.

Once out of the oven, leave them to cool for a few minutes, then enjoy them warm, and you will understand why we get a queue at the market for these babies.

BISCOTTI

These classic twice-baked biscuits are very crunchy and great to dunk in your tea or coffee. They are traditionally served with vin santo, an Italian dessert wine, which is delicious and a treat.

MAKES ABOUT 30 FRAGRANT, CRUNCHY BISCUITS

250g plain flour, plus extra for dusting

250g caster sugar, plus extra for dusting

½ teaspoon baking powder

½ teaspoon vanilla extract

2 eggs

1 egg yolk

zest of 1 orange

1 tablespoon fennel seeds

100g raisins

100g whole almonds

Preheat the oven to 180°C/fan 160°C/gas 4. Line a baking tray about 45cm x 38cm with baking paper.

Put the flour, sugar and baking powder into a bowl and mix together, then add the vanilla extract, eggs, yolk, orange zest, fennel seeds, raisins and nuts and mix by hand until everything is incorporated. Once combined into a dough, tip it on to a floured surface and roll into a sausage shape about 32–34cm long. Roll it in some sugar, dusting evenly, then place on the lined baking tray.

Place in the preheated oven and bake for 30 minutes. You want it to have a nice golden colour and still be a bit soft to the touch.

Remove from the oven, place on a cooling rack, then turn down the oven to 120°C/fan 100°C/gas ½. Allow to cool on the rack for about 10 minutes – don't leave it any longer or you won't be able to slice it very well.

When cooled, slide it on to a chopping board and cut into 1cm slices. Put the slices back on the baking tray and return it to the oven for about 40 minutes, then turn the biscotti over and bake for another 20 minutes, or until golden brown. This dries them out so that they are really, really crunchy.

Take them out of the oven and leave to cool on a rack. Once cooled, place in an airtight container and they will keep for up to 3 weeks.

PAGNOTTA

'Pagnotta' means 'loaf' in Italian. This is the big boy of the Italian chapter, with a good long bake, a cracking crust and great texture with that semolina through the dough. Do try to follow the quantities here – yes, it's big, but if you can get it into your oven, go for it. Don't be afraid to bake it dark.

The day before you want to bake your loaf, put the flour, semolina and salt into a bowl and mix them together so they get to know each other. Put the 950g of water into a separate large bowl, and weigh out the extra 90g of water into a separate container. Add the stiff and rye starters to the 950g of water, then combine the mixture as thoroughly as you can. A squeezing action with your hands really helps to break it all up.

Once incorporated, add the liquid to the flour mix and work it in for about 2 minutes. Then scrape the dough out on to a work surface dusted with semolina. Keep the bowl to one side, as you will need it later.

Now, with your dough on the work surface and you 'poised like a puma' (see page 18), with the heel of your hand push the dough into the work surface and 'stretch and tear' for about 8 minutes, using the technique described on page 18, but throughout the 8 minutes slowly adding the last 90g of water into the dough. After the first 4 minutes you will begin to feel a change in the dough as the gluten develops.

Lightly oil the bowl you used earlier and pop the dough in. Spread the oil from the bowl over the top of the dough and give the dough a fold, using the technique described on page 21. After folding, leave it to rest for an hour, then give the dough three more folds, resting for an hour each time. Between folds you will need to cover the bowl with cling film, a tea towel or a shower cap. After the final fold, cover and put into the fridge overnight.

Next day, take the dough out of the fridge and scrape it out gently on to a work surface dusted with semolina. Form into a rough ball and cover, then leave for 10 minutes. Meanwhile, line a proving basket with a folded tea towel and dust it with a mixture of semolina and flour.

Make the dough into your desired shape (see page 21), round or long, whatever shape your proving basket is. Put the dough

MAKES ONE BIG BAD BOY OF A LOAF, AND WE MEAN BIG! – ENOUGH FOR THE WHOLE FAMILY FOR A GOOD FEW DAYS

1kg strong white bread flour

300g semolina

30g salt

950g water, plus another 90g

400g stiff starter (see page 33)

100g rye starter (see page 33)

olive oil, for the bowl

semolina, for dusting

YOU WILL NEED

a water spray

into the lined basket, seam side up, and dust the top with semolina. Cover with a tea towel and leave to prove for about 6 hours.

Preheat the oven to 250°C/fan 230°C/gas 10, or as hot as it will go, and put your largest deep baking tray in to heat up. Get your water spray ready.

Gently turn out the dough on to the heated baking tray. You can slash the top with a razor blade – it looks quite nice with random slashes over the loaf. Heavily spray inside the oven with your water spray, then bake for 40–45 minutes, until a dark golden-brown crust has formed, with some singe. Take out of the oven, place on a rack to cool, and enjoy!

AMARETTI BISCUITS

I (Matt) was first introduced to these little delights when I worked with Phil Howard at the Square restaurant. They are so simple to make at home and yet so delicious.

They are like a soft, cakey biscuit with a whisper of a crunch on the outside and a real lick-o'-lip factor. We always bake more than we need for orders, because all the bakers like to eat one warm from the oven with their coffee in the morning, after the night shift.

MAKES 18 SNOWY BALLS OF JOY

2 egg whites (70g)

188g caster sugar

300g ground almonds

1½ teaspoons honey

1 teaspoon almond extract (please don't use one that's been sitting at the back of the cupboard for the last 10 years)

100g icing sugar, for dusting

Preheat the oven to 180°C/fan 160°C/gas 4, and line a couple of 45cm x 38cm baking trays with baking paper.

Place the egg whites in a bowl and whisk until frothy, then add the sugar and whisk until soft peaks are formed. This will take a good few minutes.

Add the rest of the ingredients, apart from the icing sugar, and mix with a spatula until incorporated.

Cut the dough into 18 pieces, each weighing about 30g, then roll them into balls.

Spread the icing sugar in a tray. Put the balls of dough into the tray, roll them around, then leave them to sit for 10 minutes, to absorb some of the icing sugar. Now carpet-bomb the balls with icing sugar, really packing it on.

Carefully place the sugared amaretti on the prepared baking trays, leaving a little space between them because they will puff out a bit.

Bake for 16 minutes, until golden brown, then take them out and leave them to cool a little. Perfect with an espresso.

GRISSINI

I (Matt) went to Turin a few years ago, and visited one of the few remaining factories where they still make grissini by hand. We have taken a leaf out of their book and included this in our Italian Baking class.

The night before you want to make your grissini, make your poolish. Dissolve the yeast in the water, then add to the flour in a bowl and combine fully. Cover and place in the fridge for 8–10 hours.

When you are ready to begin the dough, place your flour and salt in a large bowl and combine with one hand just enough to let the flour get to know the salt. Uncover your poolish (it will be nice and bubbly) and add to the flour.

Mix the yeast with the water, then pour into your empty poolish bowl and mix to get the last of the poolish out. Add the water and yeast to the other ingredients and start to combine, with one hand shaped like a fork. Once the dough starts to come together, take it out of the bowl and place it on a work surface sprinkled with the polenta, making sure you scrape all the dough out with a scraper to leave a clean bowl.

Now, with your dough on the work surface and you 'poised like a puma' (see page 18), with the heel of your hand push the dough into the work surface and 'stretch and tear', using the technique described on page 18, for about 6 minutes. If using, add your chopped herbs and/or seeds after the first 2 minutes. Once the dough is fully developed, cover it with a cloth and let it rest for 10 minutes.

Preheat your oven to 220°C/fan 200°C/gas 7, and line a couple of baking trays approximately 45cm x 38cm with baking paper.

Now cut the dough into 15g pieces. Roll them into short sausage shapes and let them rest for a couple more minutes. Then roll the rested dough into thin sticks about 35cm long. Once you've rolled them all out, brush them with olive oil and season with coarse sea salt.

Bake for 10 minutes, then turn the tray round and bake for a further 3 minutes, or until golden brown. Serve warm, with a dip such as pesto, or leave them to cool, then wrap prosciutto round them. They are also delicious just served crispy and plain.

MAKES 32, ABOUT 15G EACH

DAY 1: THE POOLISH (SEE PAGE 15)

2g fresh yeast

50g water

50g strong white bread flour

DAY 2

250g strong white bread flour

4g fine sea salt

4g fresh yeast

140g water

20g medium coarse polenta

optional: 1 tablespoon finely chopped herbs, e.g. chopped rosemary or thyme

optional: 1 teaspoon seeds, e.g. poppy or sesame

olive oil

coarse sea salt

FRENCH BAKING

The French think you must have fresh bread on the table no matter what time of day it is, from breakfast to dinner, and will visit the bakery sometimes two or even three times a day. Bread is a symbol of France and is born deep into their culture, from the classic baguette to the hearty pain de campagne. In France, there is strict bread legislation dictating that specific breads have to be made with certain types of yeast, flour, quantity of ingredients, and even that they have to be shaped in particular dimensions. Most towns in France, even the smaller ones, will support at least two bakeries, each closing on different days and taking different holidays, to ensure that the town will always have freshly baked bread.

In France, to be a baker is massively respected as a career, involving studying for years to get the diplomas, usually as part of a long, hard apprenticeship. They are not only bakers, but artists!

We always love going to France and joining the long queue at the local boulangerie to pick a freshly baked baguette or two. France is also famous for its beautiful, sometimes elegant and always delicious pastries – from pain au chocolat to éclairs, and this chapter will teach you how to laminate your dough to make the perfect croissant, and have you whipping up choux pastry to rival the very best Parisian pâtissiers.

THE BREAD AHEAD BAGUETTE

Where would we be without the beautiful baguette? It's a French institution, celebrated worldwide as a symbol of great baking.

In the Bread Ahead bakery we shape and bake about 500 of these baguettes every day, and when our oven is full of these beauties it is a fantastic sight! Not to mention the aroma as well. There is nothing better than a fresh-out-of-the-oven baguette spread with salted butter – ooh là là!

This is our take on the traditional French baguette, or, as one of our customers called it, the 'baguette magique' – the magic wand.

To make the first mix, weigh the flour and water into a large bowl and with one hand mix together for about 1 minute, until combined. It will still be fairly sticky, so scrape the excess off your hand back into the mix, then sprinkle or spray the top of the dough with water. Cover with cling film, a tea towel or a shower cap and leave for 1 hour.

After 1 hour, weigh the water for the second mix into a new container, add the yeast and rye starter, and mix to dissolve. Add this to the first mix, along with the salt, and again mix together with one hand. Once a loose dough is formed, take the dough out of the bowl and place on a work surface, making sure you scrape all the dough out with a scraper to leave a clean bowl. Keep the bowl to one side, as you will need it later.

Now, with your dough on the work surface and you 'poised like a puma' (see page 18), with the heel of your hand push the dough into the work surface and 'stretch and tear', using the technique described on page 18, for about 10 minutes. This will develop the elasticity within the dough and allow you to shape your baguette later.

Lightly oil the bowl you used earlier and put the dough back in. Now give it its first fold, using the technique described on page 21. After folding, leave it to rest for an hour, then give the dough two more folds, resting for an hour each time. Between folds you will need to cover the bowl with cling film, a tea towel or a shower cap.

MAKES 1 LARGE OR 2 SMALL MAGIC WANDS

FIRST MIX

440g strong white bread flour, plus extra for dusting

300g water

SECOND MIX

15g water

4g fresh yeast

70g rye starter (see page 33)

12g sea salt

olive oil, for the bowl

semolina, for dusting

YOU WILL NEED

a baking stone or an upturned baking tray

a water spray

a baker's peel or a wooden board

After the final hour's rest, tip the dough out of the bowl. It should feel lively and puffed up. Give it a gentle shape to form a round (see page 22), then cover and leave to rest for 10 minutes.

While the dough is resting, line a tray with a tea towel or couche (see page 16), and dust it with a mixture of flour and semolina.

Now it's time to shape your baguette (see page 23). You can cut your dough in half if you like, to make 2 smaller and thinner baguettes. Press the dough out to form a rectangle, then take the top of the dough, fold it over tightly with your thumbs, and repeat that action until you reach the end of the dough, sealing the bottom. If the end hasn't sealed, just pinch the dough together, making it as tight as you can as you roll it into a long baguette (but remember, it must fit into your oven, so don't make it too long!).

Place the baguette on your floured tea towel, seam side down, and wrap the towel round it. If you have made 2 baguettes, bring the towel up round one and place the other one directly next to it – the weight of each dough piece will help to hold the other's shape. Leave to prove for 20 minutes, then put into the fridge for a further 30 minutes.

Preheat your oven to 250°C/fan 230°C/gas 10, or as hot as it will go, and put a baking stone or an upturned baking tray in to heat up. Get your water spray ready.

Gently unwrap the baguette so that the seam is on the bottom and place on a semolina-dusted baker's peel or wooden board. With a razor blade, make a slash lengthways from top to bottom of the baguette, then slide it on to the baking stone or tray. Heavily spray inside the oven with your water spray, then bake for 16 minutes.

Once baked, enjoy an ooh là là moment with your baguette and some salted butter and jam.

FOUGASSE

Fougasse was traditionally used to assess the temperature of a baker's wood-fired oven, as the time it would take to bake gave the baker a pretty good idea of whether the oven temperature was hot enough for the rest of the bread to be put in.

Still popular all over France today, fougasse is delicious just on its own but even better with some toppings, like onions and herbs. I like some salty anchovies and bacon lardons on mine, for a really decadent treat. Once you are up to speed making them, try some petite versions – they are really lovely to serve as canapés and look quite beautiful.

The day before you want to bake your fougasse, make your poolish. Put the water and yeast into a bowl and mix together with your fingers or a fork until the yeast has dissolved. Add the flour and stir in until fully combined, then cover with cling film and pop into the fridge overnight.

Next day (day 2), uncover your poolish. It will have risen, plus it will be nice and bubbly and have a pleasant, slightly alcoholic aroma.

Put the three flours and the salt into a large bowl, and combine just enough to let them get to know each other. Make a well in the centre. Put the yeast and water into another bowl and stir until dissolved.

Add the poolish and the yeast and water mixture to the well in the flour, making sure you get all the yeast and liquid out of the bowl. Gently bring together with one hand until just combined, then take the dough out of the bowl and place on a floured work surface. Keep the bowl to one side, as you will need it later.

Now, with your dough on the work surface and you 'poised like a puma' (see page 18), with the heel of your hand push the dough into the work surface and 'stretch and tear', using the technique described on page 18, for about 8 minutes. After 4 minutes you will begin to feel the dough strengthen as the gluten develops. Scrape the dough back into the bowl you used earlier.

Now give your dough a fold, using the technique described on page 21. After folding, leave it to rest for 30 minutes, then give the dough three more folds, resting for 30 minutes each time.

MAKES 1 LARGE,
BEAUTIFUL FOUGASSE

DAY 1: THE POOLISH
(SEE PAGE 15)

50g water

2g fresh yeast

50g strong white
bread flour

DAY 2

250g strong white
bread flour, plus extra
for dusting

20g wholegrain flour

a pinch of rye flour (8g)

5g fine sea salt

2g fresh yeast

160g water

polenta, for dusting

olive oil, for the top

optional toppings:
herbs, sliced red onions,
lardons, anchovies

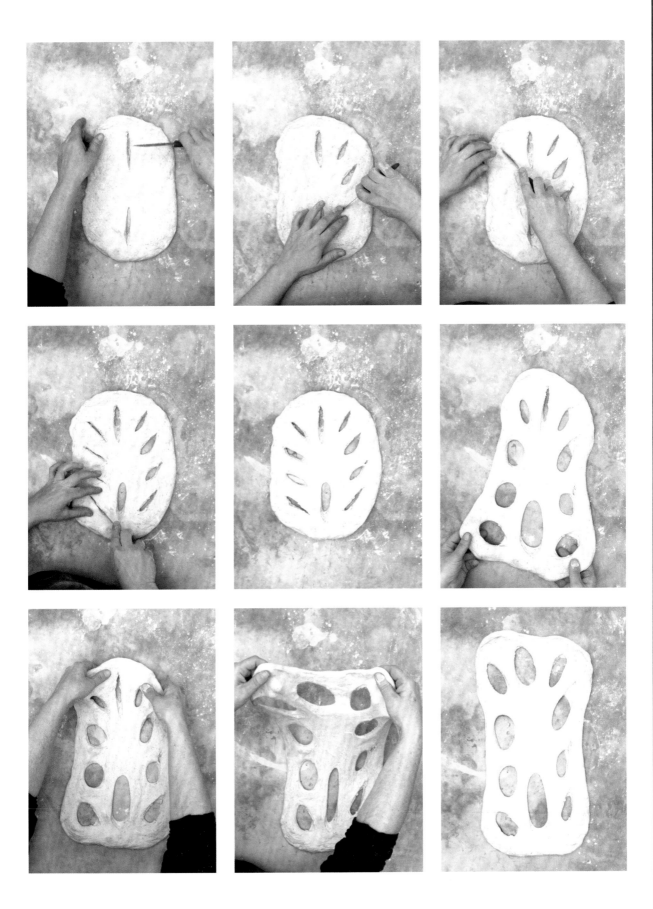

Between folds you will need to cover the bowl with cling film, a tea towel or a shower cap. After the final fold, leave for 30 minutes, then tip the dough out of the bowl on to a lightly floured work surface. It should feel lively and puffed up. Give your dough a gentle shape to form a round (see page 22), then cover and leave to rest for 10 minutes.

Now, the next step is to pat and pull your dough out to form a leaf shape. Try to be fairly gentle – this will take a few minutes, but do take your time and try not to rip the dough. When you have a leaf shape about 20cm by 25cm, take a knife and cut two slashes in the middle of the dough, then four slashes on either side of the central cuts. Pick the dough up and give it a little shake, then lay it on a polenta-lined tray. Pull the dough out to widen the slashes, then brush with olive oil and scatter over your toppings, if using. Leave to prove, uncovered, for 1 hour.

Preheat your oven to 250°C/fan 230°C/gas 10, or as hot as it will go.

After an hour, check the dough to see if the slashes have started to join together. If so, gently pull them apart. Place the fougasse in the oven and bake for 12 minutes, until golden brown. If you have put extra toppings on, it might need a minute or two longer.

Take out of the oven and serve warm. Fougasse has a lovely deep crust – it's great with soups, delicious with pesto, and looks beautiful in the middle of the dining table. All you have to do is listen out for the 'Wow's.

PAIN DE CAMPAGNE

This simple, hearty country loaf is a real beauty, with a deep flavour and a strong bake. It will grace any dinner table and goes with pretty much anything, from cold meats to just butter. Again, don't be scared of baking it dark, with some singe to the crust. It adds such a depth of flavour and sings in your mouth.

The day before you want to bake your bread, make the vieille pâte. Dissolve the yeast in the water, then combine with the flours and mix for a good 2–3 minutes. Cover with cling film or a shower cap and leave for 3 hours, just to start the fermentation process, then place in the fridge overnight or for up to 24 hours.

Next day (day 2), take your vieille pâte out of the fridge. Mix the flours and salt for the main dough in a bowl so they get to know each other. Put the water and yeast into a separate bowl and with one hand mix together so that the yeast dissolves, then add the vieille pâte. You will need to combine the two as much as you can – a squeezing action with your hands really helps to break it all up.

Once combined, add the liquid to the flour mix and work it in for about 2–3 minutes. Scrape the dough out on to a floured work surface, keeping the bowl, as you will need it later.

With your dough on the work surface and you 'poised like a puma' (see page 18), with the heel of your hand push the dough into the work surface and 'stretch and tear', using the technique described on page 18, for about 8 minutes. After the first 4 minutes you will begin to feel a change in the dough.

Now lightly oil the bowl you used earlier and pop the dough in. Spread the oil from the bowl over the top of the dough and give the dough a fold, using the technique described on page 21. After folding, leave to rest for an hour, then give the dough two more folds, resting for an hour each time. Between folds you will need to cover the bowl with cling film, a tea towel or a shower cap. After the final fold, leave for a further 30 minutes.

MAKES 1 DARK AND CRUSTY LOAF

DAY 1: THE VIEILLE PÂTE OR OLD DOUGH (SEE PAGE 15) (I PUT THE FRENCH NAME IN – IT SOUNDS SO MUCH MORE SEXY THAN 'OLD DOUGH')

2g fresh yeast

230g water

300g strong white bread flour

20g strong stoneground wholemeal flour

DAY 2

500g strong white bread flour, plus extra for dusting

40g strong stoneground wholemeal flour

16g fine sea salt

360g water

10g fresh yeast

olive oil, for the bowl

semolina, for dusting

a Dutch oven
(cast-iron casserole)
or a baking stone

a water spray

a baker's peel or
a wooden board

Line a 2kg proving basket or a large bowl, either by rubbing the inside all over with flour (wholemeal or white is fine) or lining it with a tea towel lightly dusted with flour.

Gently scrape the dough on to your work surface and shape it into a ball (see page 22). Pop the dough into the basket, seam side up, and lightly dust with flour. Place it in the fridge to rest for 2 hours, after which time it will be plumped and risen, and saying to you, 'I am ready to be baked!'

Preheat your oven to 250°C/fan 230°C/gas 10, or as hot as it will go, and put a Dutch oven (or cast-iron casserole) or baking stone in to heat up for about 10 minutes. Get your water spray ready, if you are using a baking stone.

Take the risen dough out of the fridge. If using a Dutch oven, very carefully take it out of the oven. Sprinkle the dough with semolina and gently place it top side down in the Dutch oven. Then, using a razor blade, cut a cross on the top of the dough. Put the lid on, place in the oven and bake for 35 minutes, then remove the lid and bake for a further 25 minutes.

Take the Dutch oven out and very carefully remove the loaf, then put the loaf back into the oven, directly on the oven shelf, and bake for a further 10 minutes, depending on how much singe you like.

If using a baking stone, gently and slowly turn out your dough on to a baker's peel or a wooden board, then with a razor blade slash a cross on the top and slide it off the peel on to the baking stone in the oven. Heavily spray inside the oven with your water spray and bake for 30 minutes.

After 30 minutes turn the tray round and bake for a further 10–20 minutes, depending on how much singe you like.

Remove from the oven, place on a cooling rack, and enjoy.

CROISSANTS

Croissants are all about the layers. They should be very light, really flaky and ooh, so buttery.

This 3-day recipe will have you creating your own beautiful, golden croissants at home, and once you master them there is no going back, as the flavour and texture will blow you away.

Place the flour, salt and sugar in a bowl and mix together just enough to let them get to know each other, then rub the butter into the flour. This will take about 1–2 minutes. In a separate container, dissolve the yeast in the milk and water. Once fully dissolved, pour into the flour.

Mix the ingredients together in the bowl with one hand, just enough to bring the dough together. This shouldn't take more than 1 minute. You don't want to overwork the dough, otherwise it will be harder to incorporate the butter tomorrow. Place your dough back in the bowl and push it down to form a flat disc. Cover with cling film or a shower cap, then place in the fridge for at least 8 hours and up to 12.

Next day, take the butter out of the fridge 45 minutes before you want to start work, so that it can soften. Once softened, pound it with a rolling pin to make it nice and flat. The easiest way to do this is to place it between two pieces of baking paper and gently pound it until it's about ½cm thick and about 18cm square. Cover with cling film and put back into the fridge.

Take your dough out of the fridge and place on a lightly floured work surface. Roll it out to form an 18cm square. Then, from 6cm in, roll each side to about 10cm from the middle so you have a cross with a slightly raised centre piece (photo overleaf). Brush the whole cross to remove any excess flour.

Take the butter out of the fridge again and place it in the centre of the dough, then pull each flap over to encase it. Give the dough a few little taps with your rolling pin, just to seal and flatten it. Now roll it into a rectangle about 65cm long. Brush off any excess flour, then fold it into three by bringing the top flap down by a third and folding the bottom flap over the top flap, brushing off any excess flour each time. This is called a half fold. Cover, put back into the fridge and leave to rest for 1 hour.

MAKES 12 LEGENDARY CROISSANTS

DAY 1

THE DOUGH

500g strong white bread flour, plus extra for dusting

12g fine sea salt

55g sugar

40g softened unsalted butter

30g fresh yeast

140g full fat milk

140g water

DAY 2

250g unsalted butter

1 egg, beaten, for the eggwash

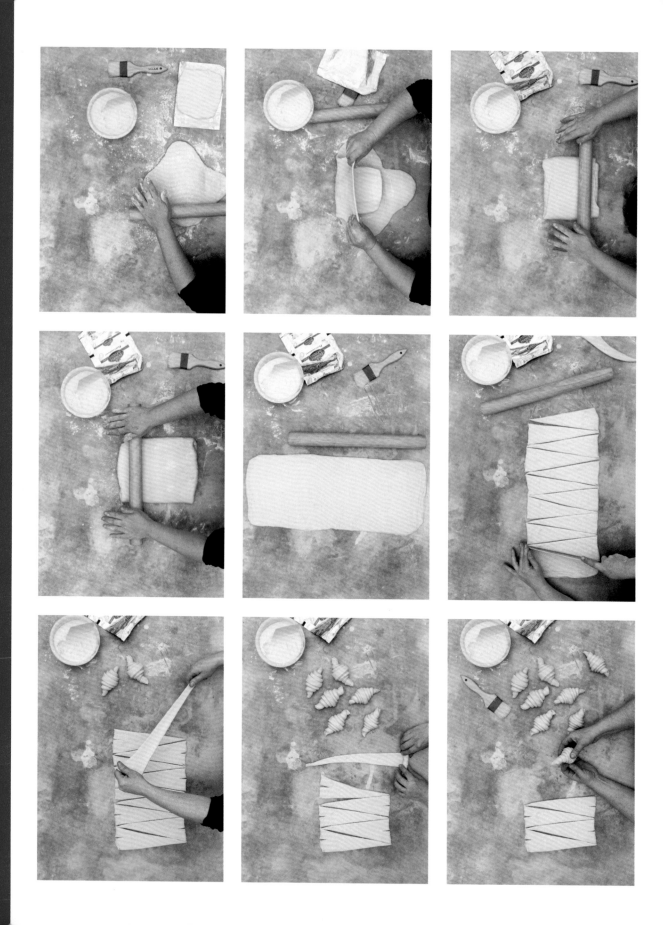

Take the dough out of the fridge and place on a lightly floured work surface. Roll it out into a rectangle about 65cm long again, give another half fold, then cover again and place in the fridge for another hour.

Repeat this one more time, so that your croissant dough has had three half folds, then place on a lightly floured tray, cover with cling film, and put back into the fridge for another hour or two. This will help hold the layers you have created in the dough (also known as lamination), and makes the dough easier to work with at the final stage.

When you're ready to shape your croissants, take the dough out of the fridge. Place on a lightly floured surface and roll out again to a good rectangle shape, about 60cm x 26cm and ½cm thick.

With a sharp knife, cut the dough into 12 equal triangles. At the bottom of each triangle make a cut about 1cm long (see picture opposite). Gently stretch out each triangle by hand, to increase the length by about 5cm.

Pull the corners either side of the cut outwards slightly then roll up your croissants, making sure the tapered 'tail' at the other end is on the bottom of the rolled-up croissant. Place them on two baking trays lined with baking paper, making sure they are evenly spaced.

Brush the eggwash all over each croissant. You can now rest your croissants in the fridge and bake them later, or, if you are ready to bake them now, leave them on the tray in a warmish place (ideally about 24°C) for about 45 minutes to 1 hour. In this time they will double in size, with a nice wobble, and you should be able to see the layers you have lovingly created. If they are not ready after 1 hour, give them a little longer – it will be worth the wait.

If you are leaving them in the fridge, give them another eggwash when they come out and remember that they will take an extra hour or so to rise up again.

Preheat your oven to 200°C/fan 180°C/gas 6.

Place the croissants in the oven and bake for 18–20 minutes. They will be a lovely golden colour, and flaky and crispy on the outside.

Take them out of the oven and enjoy. We love them served warm and plain, but if you have to, the classic butter and jam is pretty good too!

PAINS AU CHOCOLAT

The croissant's chocolatey cousin – you can't get a better breakfast!

Take the dough from the fridge (it should have been resting in the fridge overnight and had its three half folds). Place on a lightly floured work surface and roll out to a good rectangle shape, about 50cm x 38cm and ½cm thick.

   With the longest edge of the dough closest to you, fold it into thirds first from the bottom, then from the top. Cut the dough into 3 equal-sized pieces along the fold or creases – you should end up with 3 strips about 13cm wide – then cut each of these pieces into 6 equal rectangles about 8cm wide.

   Lay a chocolate stick at the top of each rectangle and roll over the dough from the top, covering the chocolate. Lay another chocolate stick next to the dough you covered the first stick with, then carry on rolling until you reach the end of the dough.

   Pop them on to a couple of baking trays lined with baking paper, seam side down, then eggwash generously and prove for about 1 hour. As in the croissants recipe on page 136, before proving you can rest them in the fridge until ready to bake, if you wish. After proving they should have doubled in size, and be puffy and pillow-like.

   Preheat your oven to 200°C/fan 180°C/gas 6.

   Bake for 20 minutes, until golden on top and oozing chocolate, and leave to cool a bit before devouring.

MAKES 18

1 batch of croissant dough, made as per instructions on page 136

plain flour, for dusting

chocolate sticks or a bar of good dark chocolate (about 70%), sliced

1 egg, beaten, for the eggwash

PAINS AUX RAISINS

The best bit is the middle!

MAKES 18

500g raisins, covered with hot tea or hot water and left overnight

plain flour, for dusting

1 batch of croissant dough, made as per instructions on page 136

250g classic vanilla custard (see page 299 – use half here, and freeze the rest for future projects)

1 egg, beaten, for the eggwash

100g caster sugar

Drain the soaked raisins, but keep the soaking liquid to one side. Take the dough out of the fridge (it should have been resting in the fridge overnight and had its three half folds). Place on a lightly floured surface and roll out to a good rectangle shape about 45cm x 40cm and ½cm thick.

Spread your vanilla custard all over the rolled-out rectangle, taking it right out to the sides, apart from 2cm along the shorter bottom edge. Sprinkle the raisins evenly over the vanilla custard (leaving the empty 2cm on the bottom), then eggwash the empty strip.

Now, from the top, roll it down like a Swiss roll, as tightly as you can, and seal at the end with the eggwash flap, rolling it back and forth to get a nice rounded shape.

Slice with a very sharp knife into 18 equal-sized pieces and gently lay them on a couple of baking trays lined with baking paper, leaving a good bit of space between them, as they will puff up and spread. Leave to prove for 1 hour. As in the croissants recipe on page 136, before proving you can rest them in the fridge until ready to bake, if you wish.

In the meantime, pour the soaking water from the raisins into a small saucepan and add the caster sugar. Bring to the boil on a high heat, then turn down and simmer until a syrup is reached. You will use this to glaze the pains aux raisins after they come out of the oven.

Preheat your oven to 200°C/fan 180°C/gas 6.

Once proved, your pains aux raisins should look puffed up and have doubled in size. Bake in the oven for 18 minutes, then swap the two trays round and bake for a further 2 minutes.

Once out of the oven, brush with your syrup, then leave to cool and devour.

ALMOND CROISSANTS

This recipe works best with slightly stale croissants, as they soak up the syrup better. Almond croissants are one of our favourite ways to use up day-old croissants at Bread Ahead, though to be honest, after you have had these for the first time, you will be making croissants just to turn them into almond croissants.

First make the frangipane. Put the butter and sugar into a large bowl and cream them together with a wooden spoon until light and fluffy. Gradually crack the eggs in one at a time, making sure each is fully mixed in before you add the next one. Then add the rest of the ingredients and mix until all is incorporated. Pop the mixture into a piping bag with a 1cm nozzle and leave to one side.

Now make the rum syrup. Put the water into a heavy-based saucepan and bring to a simmer on a medium heat, then add the sugar and heat until dissolved. Once the sugar has dissolved, take off the heat and add the rum.

Wait for the syrup to cool a little, then slice your day-old croissants with a bread knife through the front lengthways, leaving them still attached at the back. Dunk each one into the syrup for about 30 seconds, then lay them on a cooling rack. Once they are all soaked, put them on a baking tray lined with baking paper.

Preheat your oven to 180°C/fan 160°C/gas 4.

Pipe a couple of lines of frangipane inside the croissants and a little line on top, then stick some flaked almonds on top. Bake the croissants for about 30 minutes, or until the frangipane inside has baked. Have a little peek after 25 minutes by carefully lifting up a croissant and looking inside – if it is still runny and unbaked, pop them back in for a few more minutes until the frangipane has set.

Once baked they should be looking gorgeous and smelling even better. Dust with icing sugar and enjoy warm.

MAKES 12

1 batch of 12 croissants (see page 136), 1–2 days old

THE FRANGIPANE

250g softened unsalted butter

250g caster sugar

5 eggs

250g ground almonds

3 teaspoons almond essence

25g plain white flour, sifted

a pinch of salt

THE RUM SYRUP

1kg water

500g caster sugar

100g dark rum

TO DECORATE

flaked almonds

icing sugar

YOU WILL NEED

a piping bag fitted with a 1cm nozzle

CHEESE AND HAM CROISSANTS

Again, this recipe works best with slightly stale croissants. We started to do these cheese and ham versions for Bastille Day at Borough Market, and they always sell out in the first few hours. This is another way of using up any leftover croissants by transforming them into something quite special and very delicious.

MAKES 12

1 batch of 12 croissants (see page 136), 1–2 days old

12 slices of really delicious ham

300g mature Cheddar cheese, grated

100g smoked bacon lardons

500ml chicken stock (see method)

optional: chopped parsley

MRS G'S WHITE SAUCE

1 litre full fat milk

1 small onion, peeled and sliced

20 black peppercorns

15 whole cloves

4 bay leaves

80g unsalted butter

80g plain white flour

5g powdered English mustard

2 teaspoons fine sea salt

To make the white sauce, put the milk, sliced onion, peppercorns, cloves and bay leaves into a heavy-based saucepan. Bring to a slow simmer, then leave to simmer for a few minutes, to infuse all those great flavours. Give it a stir a few times so you don't catch the milk on the bottom of the pan, then take off the heat and set aside.

In another heavy-based saucepan, melt the butter on a low heat. Once melted, add the flour and mustard, stir to incorporate, and cook gently for 4–5 minutes to cook out the flour (don't let it burn).

Pass the milk through a fine sieve, then start to add it slowly to the butter and flour mix, about 100ml at a time. Stir into the flour, then once fully incorporated repeat until all the milk is in and fully combined. Now bring to the boil and simmer for 2 minutes, stirring continuously.

Take off the heat and pour into a bowl, then whisk in the salt. Lay a sheet of cling film directly on top of the sauce to stop a skin forming, and leave to cool.

Now make the chicken stock. Put all the ingredients into a pan and cover with water. Bring to the boil, then reduce the heat and simmer for 20 minutes. Pass through a fine sieve and leave to cool a little.

Slice your day-old croissants with a bread knife through the front lengthways, leaving them still attached at the back. Dunk each one into the stock for about 10 seconds, then lay them on a cooling rack. Once they have all been soaked, pop them on to a baking tray lined with baking paper.

Spread a good heaped tablespoon of white sauce on the bottom half of each cut croissant, then fold a slice of ham in half and lay it on top of the white sauce. Add a bit of grated cheese to each one, setting aside 100g of cheese to finish the croissants.

Close the croissants and top them evenly with the remaining white sauce. Sprinkle them with the uncooked lardons and the rest of the cheese.

At this point you can put them into the fridge, where they will be happy for 3–4 days. When ready to bake, preheat your oven to 180°C/fan 160°C/gas 4. Pop them into the oven for 15 minutes, then turn the heat up to 200°C/fan 180°C/gas 6, turn the trays round and bake for a further 10 minutes. The croissants should be piping hot, crispy on top and oozing and unctuous in the middle.

Leave to cool a little, sprinkle some chopped parsley on top if you want to, and enjoy.

THE CHICKEN STOCK

1 chicken carcass

1 onion, roughly chopped

1 leek, roughly chopped

1 carrot, roughly chopped

4 cloves of garlic, roughly chopped

12 peppercorns

4 bay leaves

2 sprigs of fresh thyme

CLASSIC BRIOCHE

This soft bread is enriched with butter, lots of butter, actually a whole pack, but it's well worth it. When the brioche comes out of the oven and floods the air with its sweet buttery aroma, it's one of the best smells in the bakery.

The list of different shapes you can turn your brioche into is endless, from the classic 'tête', using lovely fluted shaped moulds, to a golden plaited loaf or a simple tin.

Brioche is a fantastic accompaniment to many dishes, and also toasts up a treat for serving with pâté.

MAKES 2 X 550G LOAVES

500g strong white bread flour, plus extra for dusting

12g fine sea salt

30g caster sugar

15g fresh yeast

6 eggs

250g softened unsalted butter, plus extra for greasing

1 egg, beaten, for the eggwash

Put the flour, salt and sugar into a bowl and mix together just enough for the flour to meet the salt and sugar. Crumble in the yeast and mix in, then pour in the eggs and mix together with one hand. As you mix it will become a firm dough, and you might find some flour not mixing in – but don't worry if that happens, just pour it out on to your work surface and scrape the remaining dough out of the bowl and off your hand.

Now, with your dough on the work surface and you 'poised like a puma' (see page 18), with the heel of your hand push the dough into the work surface and 'stretch and tear', using the technique described on page 18, for about 5 minutes. Cover with a tea towel and leave to rest for 2 minutes.

Butter time! Cut the butter into quarters. Break the first quarter of the butter into little pieces and place all over the brioche dough. Again 'poised like a puma', with the heel of your hand push the dough into the work surface and 'stretch and tear' to incorporate the butter. This should take about 1½ minutes per quarter. Make sure you scrape your dough to the centre throughout so that the butter is mixed through evenly. When all the butter has been incorporated, form your dough into a ball (see page 22).

The dough should now be glossy, smooth and elastic when pulled. Dust the inside of the bowl with flour, then put the dough back into the bowl. Cover with cling film and leave until it has doubled in size (this will take 1–2 hours). Place in the fridge overnight to chill.

Next day, grease two 20cm x 10cm x 6cm loaf tins. Take the dough out of the fridge, divide it in half, and mould each one into a loaf shape. Place in your prepared tins, pressing the dough down into each corner. Cover, then leave somewhere warm to prove. The dough needs to prove until it reaches the top of the tin (well, just a bit prouder than the top), which will take about 2–2½ hours.

Preheat your oven to 180°C/fan 160°C/gas 4.

Brush the brioche with the eggwash and bake for 20 minutes, then take out of the tin and put back into the oven, directly on the oven shelf, for another 5 minutes.

Place on a rack to cool a little and serve warm or toasted.

ORANGE + LEMON SUGARED BRIOCHE BUNS / MAKES 12

These light sugared fragrant buns are lovely and light.
Fill them with ice cream for a summer delight.

½ a batch of brioche, after the butter is added (see page 151) / 100g mixed peel / zest of 3 oranges / zest of 2 lemons / plain flour, for dusting / 1 egg, beaten, for the eggwash / granulated sugar, for the topping

After you have added the butter to your brioche dough, add the mixed peel and citrus zests and mix in. Dust the inside of the bowl with flour, then put the dough back into the bowl, cover with cling film and leave until it has doubled in size (this will take about 1–2 hours). Put into the fridge overnight to chill.

Next morning, divide the dough into 12 equal pieces, roll them into balls and place on a lined baking tray, leaving space between them. Cover, then leave somewhere warm to prove until they double in size, which will take about 1–2 hours.

Preheat the oven to 180°C/fan 160°C/gas 4.

Brush the brioche buns with the eggwash, dust with granulated sugar and bake for 8 minutes, then turn the tray round and bake for a further 4 minutes. Place on a rack to cool a little, and serve warm or toasted.

BAY LEAF + LARDON BRIOCHE BUN SCROLLS / MAKES 15

A match made in heaven, swirl-tastic!
Great with soup and cheeky in a lunchbox.

400g smoked lardons / 4 sprigs of rosemary /
10 bay leaves / 10 cloves of garlic, peeled and crushed /
4 banana shallots, peeled and finely sliced /
½ a batch of brioche (see page 151), after its overnight prove /
plain flour, for dusting / 1 egg, beaten, for the eggwash

Place the lardons, rosemary and bay leaves in a saucepan on a medium heat with no oil. Cook gently for about 10 minutes, until starting to colour, then add the crushed garlic and sliced shallots and continue to cook until soft. This should take about 4–5 minutes, stirring occasionally. Once cooked, place in a bowl, cover and chill overnight.

Next day, take the dough out of the fridge and put it on a floured surface, then, with a rolling pin, roll it out into a 40cm x 25cm rectangle. Spread the bay leaf and bacon mix all over, pretty much right to the ends.

Time to roll, so with the shortest end nearest to you, start to roll it up like a Swiss roll. Try to roll it as tightly and neatly as possible. Wrap the roll in cling film and put it into the fridge for 10 minutes to firm up. Take out and place on a board, then take a sharp knife and slice it into about 15 even pieces.

Place the slices on a baking tray lined with baking paper, leaving space between them. Cover, then leave somewhere warm to prove until they look nice and puffed up and start to touch each other, which will take about 1–2 hours.

Preheat the oven to 200°C/fan 180°C/gas 6.

Brush the brioche with the eggwash and bake for 10 minutes until golden brown.

Put on a rack to cool a little and serve warm or toasted. These rolls are delicious on their own with butter, and fantastic with a lovely bowl of soup.

BEURRE NOISETTE (BROWN BUTTER) MADELEINES

I once said that you can use a muffin tray for madeleines if you have to, but NO, you should treat yourself to a madeleine tray – you want that raised 'nipple' on the top.

Remember to serve them straight from the oven, steaming hot – this is a real 'moment' in life.

Put the butter into a small saucepan and melt on a low heat. When it starts to foam, stir it continuously to stop the milk solids burning. When it turns brown and smells nutty and toasty, pour it into a bowl and add the honey. Stir together, then pass through a fine sieve and leave to cool a little.

Place the eggs and both sugars in a bowl and whisk using an electric mixer for about 5 minutes, until tripled in volume. Fold in the melted butter and honey. Once incorporated, add the sifted flour and baking powder and fold in again until all is incorporated, trying not to knock too much air out of the mixture. Put into the fridge to rest for at least 4 hours, and ideally overnight.

Preheat the oven to 200°C/fan 180°C/gas 6. Grease and flour your madeleine tray, tapping out any excess flour.

Now stir the mixture to bring it all together (yes, that's right – you will lose the air but that's fine, trust me).

Spoon about 1 tablespoon of the mixture (30–32g) into each mould, so that it is almost level with the rim, and bake for 10 minutes. Then turn the tray round and bake for a further 2 minutes. Take the tray out of the oven, admire those nipples, and eat straight away while still hot. OMG!

MAKES ABOUT 18 PERKED NIPPLED MADELEINES

205g unsalted butter (to make 165g of brown butter)

45g clear honey

4 eggs

150g caster sugar

20g demerara sugar

160g plain flour, sifted, plus extra for dusting

10g baking powder

softened butter and plain flour, for the tray

YOU WILL NEED
a madeleine tray

COCO AU MIEL (COCONUT HONEY CAKES)

Justin first encountered these in a small-town bakery in France, and thought they were quite special. These are our version, which we make at Bread Ahead.

MAKES 20

310g full fat milk

1½ teaspoons honey

1 teaspoon coconut oil

zest of 1 orange

1 vanilla pod

250g shredded coconut

125g caster sugar

75g plain flour

2 teaspoons baking powder

2 large eggs

1 egg yolk

Put the milk, honey, coconut oil, orange zest and vanilla pod into a saucepan and bring to a light simmer, then remove from the heat.

In a large bowl, mix together the shredded coconut, sugar, flour and baking powder, then slowly add the milk mixture and stir together. Now beat in the eggs and egg yolk, one at a time. Once they are all beaten in, cover the bowl and pop it into the fridge overnight.

Next day, preheat your oven to 220°C/fan 200°C/gas 7. Take the mixture out of the fridge, spoon 40g into each of 20 cupcake cases, and pop them on to a cardboard-lined baking tray (the cardboard will protect the bottom so they don't burn).

Bake for 15 minutes – you want them dark on top so you get that contrast of flavours.

Leave to cool, and enjoy with a strong coffee.

CHOUX PASTRY

Choux pastry is used for classics such as profiteroles, éclairs and gougères. Unlike other pastries, it doesn't follow those basic rules like 'cream your butter and sugar together' or 'rub the flour and butter together' – the technique in this recipe is very particular to choux.

Put the butter, water, milk, salt and sugar into a heavy-based saucepan and place over a medium heat until the butter has melted.

Turn up the heat and bring to the boil, then take off the heat and stir in the sifted flour. Put back on the heat and cook for about 1 minute. This is to cook out the flour and to dry your paste a little.

Put the paste into a bowl and leave to cool for about 10 minutes.

Now beat the eggs and start to add them to the bowl, whisking them in about one at a time (waiting until each is completely mixed in before adding the next one), until they're all incorporated and the mixture is glossy and smooth.

Now use for any of the recipes over the page.

125g unsalted butter

125g water

125g full fat milk

3g fine sea salt

5g caster sugar

150g strong white bread flour, sifted

4 eggs

1 egg, beaten, for the eggwash

YOU WILL NEED

a piping bag fitted with a 1½–2cm plain or star nozzle

PARIS-BREST

Paris-Brest is a crispy, creamy French choux pastry dessert that takes its name from the Paris–Brest–Paris cycling race. Its circular shape resembles a bicycle wheel. Traditionally a Paris-Brest is filled with praline cream, but we use a coffee cream custard in this version.

MAKES 1 – SERVES 6–8
DINNER GUESTS OR 4
GREEDY ONES

1 batch of choux pastry
(see page 158)

1 egg, beaten, for
the eggwash

flaked almonds

coffee cream custard
(see page 162)

icing sugar, for dusting

YOU WILL NEED
a piping bag fitted with
a 14mm star nozzle

Preheat your oven to 180°C/fan 160°C/gas 4.

Draw a 20cm circle on a sheet of baking paper, then turn it over so the pencil mark is on the underside and lay it on a baking tray.

Put a 14mm star nozzle into a piping bag and pipe two rings of choux pastry on to your sheet. Start with the largest ring, round the edge of the 20cm circle marking, then pipe the second ring directly inside the first ring, both touching.

Now pipe a third ring on top, in the middle of the first two rings. Gently brush the eggwash over your rings of choux and cover with flaked almonds. Use the rest of the mixture to pipe out some small profiteroles (see page 165) and sprinkle them with flaked almonds.

Bake the profiteroles in the oven for about 26 minutes. Bake your choux ring for 40 minutes, then turn up the heat to 200°C/fan 180°C/gas 6 and bake for a further 10 minutes.

Remove from the oven and place on a cooling rack. When the pastry has cooled, slice through the choux ring horizontally with a bread knife, forming two rings. Turn over the top ring so you can see the inside, then pop both rings back into the oven at 180°C/fan 160°C/gas 4 for 8 minutes, just to crisp them up a little more.

Place on a cooling rack. Once cool, pipe most of your coffee cream custard round the bottom half of the choux ring, and top with the other half of the ring. Fill the centre with some of the small profiteroles and use the rest of the coffee cream custard to stick them all round the top of the ring (see page 159). Dust with icing sugar and eat straight away!

COFFEE CREAM CUSTARD /
MAKES ENOUGH FOR 1 PARIS-BREST

500g full fat milk / 25g good happy rich ground coffee / 6 egg yolks /
70g caster sugar / 50g soft dark brown sugar / 40g plain white flour /
125g double cream / 15g soft light brown sugar

Put the milk and coffee into a heavy-based saucepan and slowly bring
to the boil, to infuse the coffee. Meanwhile, mix the egg yolks, caster
and dark brown sugar in a bowl, then sift in the flour, whisking but not
for too long – just enough to mix them together.

Turn up the heat so the milk comes to the boil, then pour it on to
the egg yolk mix and whisk together. Pour it back into the saucepan,
place back on a medium heat and whisk just for 2–3 minutes – this
will help to cook out the flour and thicken up the custard.

Pass it through a fine mesh sieve into a bowl, then lay some cling
film on the surface and leave to cool. Whip the cream and light brown
sugar to stiff peaks and fold into the cooled coffee custard.

ÉCLAIRS / MAKES ABOUT 30

The French word for lightning, these will go in a flash!

1 batch of choux pastry (see page 158) / 1 egg, beaten, for the eggwash

YOU WILL NEED
a piping bag fitted with a 12mm star nozzle

Preheat the oven to 180°C/fan 160°C/gas 4.

Pipe the choux pastry in 10cm long finger shapes, leaving some
space between them, as they will spread a little. Brush with the
eggwash and bake for 28 minutes, until crisp and golden brown, then
place on a cooling rack.

Once cool, fill with your desired filling (try the classic vanilla custard
on page 299 or the coffee cream custard above).

SESAME GOUGÈRES / MAKES ABOUT 40

These are delicious served hot straight out of the oven,
with a chilled glass of wine.

_____

125g Gruyère cheese / 1 batch of choux pastry (see page 158) /
1 egg, beaten, for the eggwash / 50g sesame seeds /
crunchy sea salt flakes and freshly ground black pepper

YOU WILL NEED
a piping bag fitted with a 12mm star nozzle

Preheat your oven to 180°C/fan 160°C/gas 4.

Mix the cheese into the choux pastry. Put a 12mm star nozzle into
a piping bag and pipe the choux pastry in 4cm rounds (if they have a
little peak, press it down with a damp finger), leaving some space
between them, as they will spread a little. You should be able to make
40 gougères.

Brush them with the eggwash, then sprinkle with the sesame seeds, a
good few twists of black pepper and a sprinkle of crunchy sea salt flakes.

Bake for 24 minutes, until golden brown and deliciously cheesy.

Serve straight away and eat while warm.

PROFITEROLES / MAKES ABOUT 40

Don't forget the chocolate sauce!

_____

1 batch of choux pastry (see page 158) / 1 egg, beaten, for the eggwash / icing sugar, for dusting

CHOCOLATE SAUCE
500g chocolate (70%) / 700g water / 120g caster sugar

YOU WILL NEED
a piping bag fitted with a 12mm star nozzle

Preheat the oven to 180°C/fan 160°C/gas 4.

Pipe the choux pastry in 4cm rounds (if they have a little peak, press it down with a damp finger), leaving some space between them, as they will spread a little. You should be able to make 40 profiteroles. Brush them with the eggwash and bake for 26 minutes until crisp and golden brown, then place on a cooling rack.

Once cool, fill with your desired filling (try the classic vanilla custard on page 299 or the coffee cream custard on page 162), dust with icing sugar, and serve with chocolate sauce (see below).

CHOCOLATE SAUCE: Place all the ingredients in a saucepan and slowly bring to a gentle simmer, whisking every few minutes. Pass through a fine sieve.

THE SWAN / MAKES 20 SWANS AND 12 CYGNETS

These are absolutely stunning, and not too hard to do.

_____

1 batch of choux pastry (see page 158) /
classic vanilla custard (see page 299) / icing sugar, for dusting

YOU WILL NEED
a piping bag, plus various star nozzles

Preheat your oven to 200°C/fan 180°C/gas 6.

Using a fine nozzle, pipe the choux pastry into the shape of a figure 2 on some baking paper on a baking tray – it should be about 8cm high for the swans and 5cm high for the cygnets. The best way to do this is to mark out 8cm and 5cm on your baking paper. These will be the heads and necks of your swans and cygnets. Do more than you need, as there are always a few casualties, i.e. broken necks! Pipe a little teardrop on top of your figure 2 to provide a head.

Bake in the preheated oven for about 3–4 minutes, until golden brown, watching them carefully, as they burn easily. Once baked, leave to cool on the tray.

While they are cooling, you need to pipe the bodies, using a 12mm star nozzle. Pipe up, then come back over to produce a tail. You can make smaller bodies just by attaching a smaller nozzle over the large one (so you don't have to use another piping bag).

Now bake the swans for 22 minutes, and any cygnets you've made for just 16 minutes.

Once out of the oven, leave to cool on the tray.

Now to make your swans! First slice the body of each swan lengthways and horizontally with a very sharp knife to take the top off, at a downward angle to the tail. Slice the tops that you have removed in half again lengthways. These will form the wings.

Using a star nozzle, pipe some classic vanilla custard into the open body of each swan. Stick the wings in on either side, then gently pop the neck on top. Lastly, with a whisper of a shake, dust your swans with icing sugar. You can also dust one with cocoa powder to make an ugly duckling.

AMERICAN BAKING

A lot of what we think of as American baking comes from many different influences, from the British first bringing their wheat to Massachusetts, to the Italians for their pizzas, the Dutch for their doughnuts, the Germans for their pretzels and the Jewish community for their bagels.

Yet many of the baked goods we eat today were invented in America and have since spread all over the world – for example, burger buns. They were developed in the US in 1916 by the fry cook Walter Anderson. Five years later he went on to co-found the world's first burger chain, White Castle. Today in the US they get through 50 billion burgers each year. That's a lot of bun action! Even at Bread Ahead, though on a smaller scale, demand is such that we have an entire shift dedicated to our brioche style burger buns.

When talking about bread in the US, most bakers begin with the San Francisco bread movement, with its unique sourdough starter, originally made by local gold miners in the early 1800s. We've heard there is a bakery in San Francisco that opened in 1849 and is still using the same sourdough starter today!

In 1928 the Chillicothe Baking Company in Missouri started to sell the first white sliced bread made using a bread-slicing machine. Two years later the 'Wonder Bread' was born and became America's first nationally distributed bread.

But recently, just like in England, the baking revolution has started. Many micro and small bakeries are opening up their doors and bringing the old skills back, from shaping and rolling by hand to using ancient grains and long fermentation to bake bread with flavour, restoring the passion and the love to the loaf.

NEW YORK BAGELS

When we think of bagels, thoughts of smoked salmon and cream cheese always come to mind too. Justin's first encounter with a bagel was at about 3 a.m. at the famous 24-hour bagel shop on Brick Lane, in London. It was packed with salt beef and a drop of mustard, well, a bucketload of mustard, and it was absolutely fantastic. This is our recipe for classic, NYC-style bagels.

In a large bowl, dissolve the yeast and malt syrup in the water.

Add the flour and salt and combine just enough to bring the dough together. Tip it out on to your work surface and 'stretch and tear' (see page 18) for 6 minutes, to develop the gluten, then shape into a ball and pop it into a lightly oiled bowl. Cover with cling film or a shower cap and leave to prove for 1 hour.

Cut the dough into 13 or 14 pieces, each about 110g, shape them into rounds, then cover with a tea towel and leave to rest for 10 minutes on your work surface.

Shape into bagels, either by rolling the pieces of dough into 25cm long sausages, bringing the two ends together and sealing, or by rolling the pieces into balls, sticking one finger through the middle and twisting until it leaves a hole in the centre. Place on a tray, leaving plenty of space between them so that they don't stick together, cover, then leave to prove briefly again for about 10 minutes.

Meanwhile, put the sugar into a large, heavy-based saucepan with 4 litres of water. Bring to the boil, then reduce the heat to a simmer.

Preheat the oven to 240°C/fan 220°C/gas 9. Line two baking trays with oiled baking paper.

Poaching time: gently lift up your bagels and pop them into the simmering water. Don't crowd the saucepan, do it in a few batches. Poach your bagels for approximately 20 seconds on each side, 40 seconds total, and put them on the lined baking trays, spacing them out evenly.

Using a fork, beat the egg white lightly, then liberally brush your bagels with it and sprinkle with seeds if desired. Bake for 10 minutes, then turn the tray round and bake for a further 6 minutes, until the bagels are a golden-brown colour.

MAKES 13–14

25g fresh yeast

14g malt syrup

540g cold water

925g strong white bread flour

14g fine sea salt

oil, for greasing

60g caster sugar (you can substitute honey if you like)

egg white, for brushing

optional: poppy, sesame and mustard seeds, for the top

NEW YORK PRETZELS

These guys were brought to the shores of Bread Ahead by Sim Cass, one of our bakery school teachers.

Today an American staple, pretzels were originally made by European monks in the Middle Ages, their shape supposedly resembling the crossed arms of a person at prayer.

MAKES 8–9

12g fresh yeast

45g olive oil

4 good splashes of hot sauce (such as Tabasco)

455g cold water

750g strong white bread flour

14g fine sea salt

oil, for greasing

60g caster sugar (you can substitute honey if you like)

egg white, for brushing

crunchy sea salt flakes, for sprinkling

In a large bowl, dissolve the yeast, olive oil and hot sauce in the water.

Add the flour and salt, then combine just enough to bring the dough together. Tip it out on to your work surface and 'stretch and tear' (see page 18) for 8 minutes, to develop the gluten, then shape it into a ball and pop it into a lightly oiled bowl. Cover with cling film or a shower cap and leave to prove for 1 hour.

Cut the dough into 8 or 9 pieces, about 140g each, shape them into rounds, then cover and leave to rest for 5 minutes.

Preheat the oven to 240°C/fan 220°C/gas 9. Line two baking trays with oiled baking paper.

Roll the pieces of dough into 70cm lengths and fold each one into a pretzel shape (see pictures). Place your pretzels on a floured tray, cover with a tea towel and leave to prove for 5 minutes.

Meanwhile, put the sugar into a large, heavy-based saucepan with 4 litres of water. Bring to the boil, then reduce the heat to a simmer.

Poaching time: gently lift up your pretzels and pop them into the simmering water. Don't crowd the pan, do it in batches. Poach your pretzels for approximately 10 seconds on each side, total 20 seconds, then put them on the lined baking trays, spacing them out evenly.

Using a fork, beat the egg white lightly, then brush the pretzels with it and sprinkle with crunchy sea salt. Bake for 14–15 minutes, until a golden-brown colour is achieved.

Once baked, place on a rack to cool. Serve with mustard.

BURGER BUNS, HOT DOG BUNS AND SLIDER BUNS

These are perfect for your burgers and hot dogs, but are also great as lunchtime rolls or in a packed lunch. They freeze really well after baking, so they are a great thing to have up your sleeve. Justin made these buns for Prince William and Kate's wedding in 2011 – they served them as bacon buns in the morning.

Line a baking tray with baking paper.

Measure the flour, salt and sugar into a bowl and combine. Make a well in the centre.

In another bowl, add the yeast to the water and mix until dissolved. Pour the liquid into the well in the flour, then gently bring the dough together. Once it starts coming together, take it out of the bowl and place it on your work surface (but don't add any extra flour).

Now, with your dough on the work surface and you 'poised like a puma' (see page 18), with the heel of your hand push the dough into the work surface and 'stretch and tear', using the technique described on page 18, for about 6–8 minutes.

Sprinkle the dough with a little flour and let it rest in a bowl for 10 minutes – you can leave it uncovered. After resting, return the dough to your work surface and slowly add the butter, a little at a time, in pieces of about 25g, as you continue to 'stretch and tear' the dough. Continue until all the butter is incorporated, being careful not to add it too quickly.

Once the butter is incorporated, continue to 'stretch and tear' for another 1 minute, then return the dough to the bowl, cover and let it rest for another 10 minutes.

Divide up your dough, depending on what you feel like baking. For burger buns, cut it into 60g pieces. For sliders, cut it into 40g pieces, or for really cool mini ones 25g. For hot dog buns or lobster rolls, cut it into 100g pieces, or for smaller versions try 60g. You'll be able to make 12 x 100g, 15 x 80g, 20 x 60g, 30 x 40g and 48 x 25g.

MAKES 20 X 60G BUNS

600g strong white bread flour, plus extra for dusting

11g fine sea salt

44g caster sugar

22g fresh yeast

330g cold water

100g softened unsalted butter

1 egg, beaten, for the eggwash

optional: mustard seeds or sesame seeds, for the top

Once you have divided up your dough, roll the pieces into balls or into long buns for hot dogs (remember to make them a little bigger/longer than your filling). Place them on the prepared baking tray, leaving some space between them. Cover loosely with cling film and leave to prove until doubled in size (about 1–2 hours).

Preheat your oven to 200°C/fan 180°C/gas 6.

Brush the tops of the buns with eggwash and if sprinkling with seeds, do it now.

Bake for about 6 minutes for 25–40g buns, 8 minutes for 60g buns, and about 10 minutes for 80–100g buns. When baked, they should be golden-brown and glorious! Before removing from the oven, make sure the bottoms of the buns are a nice lightly golden brown colour too.

Put on a rack to cool for a few minutes, then cut in half and fill with your desired filling. Get messy and enjoy.

ANADAMA BREAD

This traditional bread, popular in New England, is made with cornmeal as well as bread flour. There are a few different stories told about how this bread got its name. My favourite version is that there was a man who would find cornmeal mush in his tin lunch pail every day, despite asking his loving wife for a piece of bread instead. One day, because of bad weather, he came home just before lunchtime. His wife, Anna, was out. He sat down and opened his lunchbox to find the usual cornmeal mush. He sighed and said, 'Anna, damn her,' then reached for the flour, molasses and yeast, which he added to the cornmeal mush. His resulting bread became a local favourite.

First dissolve the yeast in the milk and whisk in the melted butter.

In a large bowl, mix the flour, cornmeal, sugar and salt together just enough for them to get to know each other, then add the milk mixture.

With one hand shaped like a fork, gently bring the mixture together until just combined. Scrape the dough off your hand into the bowl, then take out the dough and place it on a work surface, making sure you scrape all the dough out with a scraper to leave a clean bowl. Keep the bowl to one side, as you will need it later.

Now, with your dough on the work surface and you 'poised like a puma' (see page 18), with the heel of your hand push the dough into the work surface and 'stretch and tear', using the technique described on page 18, for about 5 minutes. Form lightly into a ball and pop it into the lightly oiled bowl you used earlier.

You now need to fold the dough, using the technique described on page 21. After folding, leave to rest for 30 minutes, then give the dough two more folds, resting for 30 minutes each time. Between folds you will need to cover the bowl with cling film, a tea towel or a shower cap. After the final fold, cover and leave for a further 30 minutes.

Grease a loaf tin 20cm x 10cm x 6cm with butter and sprinkle coarse cornmeal/polenta all over the inside.

Cut 140g pieces of dough, roll them into smooth tight balls, and squeeze them into the tin. Heavily sprinkle with more cornmeal/polenta, then cover with a shower cap or tea towel

MAKES 1 SMALL LOAF, BEST EATEN WARM ON DAY OF BAKING

3g fresh yeast

225g full fat milk

36g unsalted butter, melted, plus extra for greasing

285g strong white bread flour

100g cornmeal flour

50g soft dark brown sugar

5g fine sea salt

sunflower oil, for the bowl

coarse cornmeal/ polenta, for dusting

YOU WILL NEED

a water spray

and leave to prove until the dough comes up to about 2cm above the top of the tin, which will take about 4 hours.

Preheat the oven to 240°C/fan 220°C/gas 9. Get your water spray ready.

Once proved, uncover your loaf and put it into the preheated oven. With your water spray on fine mist, spray lightly inside the oven, then bake the loaf for about 35 minutes. Take out and remove from the tin, then pop back into the oven, directly on the oven shelf, and bake for an extra 5 minutes. It should be golden all over. If not, put back into the oven for another few minutes.

When ready, place on a cooling rack, and serve warm.

CORNBREAD / SERVES 8–12

The southern American daily bread, fantastic at any barbecue.

200g yellow cornmeal or polenta flour / 100g plain flour, sifted / 2 teaspoons baking powder / 1 teaspoon onion powder / 1 teaspoon garlic powder / 2 teaspoons sugar / 1 teaspoon salt / 50g mature Cheddar cheese, grated / 100g sweetcorn / 4 spring onions, finely sliced / 1 tablespoon chopped jalapeños / 60g unsalted butter, melted to nut brown, plus extra for greasing / 250ml milk / 100ml buttermilk / 2 eggs

Preheat your oven to 180°C/fan 160°C/gas 4. Grease a 30cm x 20cm x 4cm baking tin and line it with baking paper.

In a large bowl, mix together the cornmeal, plain flour, baking powder, onion and garlic powder, sugar, salt, cheese, sweetcorn, spring onions and jalapeños, then stir in the brown butter.

Beat together the milk, buttermilk and eggs, and stir into the cornmeal mixture to make a smooth batter.

Pour into your lined tin and bake for 40 minutes, until set and golden brown.

Turn out of the tin, cut into slices and serve warm.

BROWNIES

Dark, rich and moist, and loved all over the world. We make huge amounts of these brownies, with a towering stack always for sale on our stall in Borough Market.

Try adding extra things to the mix, like nuts, sour cherries or salted crisp pretzels.

Preheat your oven to 180°C/fan 160°C/gas 4. Lightly grease a 38cm x 25cm x 2cm baking tray and line it with baking paper.

Put the butter and chocolate into a heatproof bowl over a pan of lightly simmering water and leave to melt slowly.

While the chocolate is melting, whisk the eggs, malt syrup and sugar together in a large bowl for about 3–4 minutes.

Once the chocolate has melted, pour it over the egg mix and whisk together briefly. Fold in the sifted flour, cocoa and salt.

Pour the mixture into the prepared baking tray and bake for 20 minutes, then turn the tray round and bake for a further 8 minutes. Take it out of the oven and place on a cooling rack for 1 hour – it might look a little under-baked, but as it cools down it will firm up.

Serve warm, with ice cream, or (our favourite) put it into the fridge overnight and eat chilled as a chocolate bar.

MAKES ABOUT 20

300g unsalted butter, plus extra for greasing

500g chocolate, broken up

6 eggs

100g malt syrup

500g caster sugar

125g plain flour, sifted

15g cocoa powder

1 teaspoon fine sea salt

THE PICKLEBACK AND CARAWAY NEW YORK RYE

The Pickleback is a drink in the US where you chase a shot of whiskey with a shot of pickle brine. When Justin tried it for the first time, after a couple – or four! – he started thinking about what else we could use pickle brine in, and our pickleback and caraway New York rye was born.

Use it to make a sandwich packed with thinly sliced pastrami and mustard, with a pickle on the side.

Place the flours, caraway seeds and salt in a large bowl, and mix together just enough for them to get to know each other. Pour the pickle brine and rye starter into a separate bowl, then mix together to combine and break up the starter a little.

Pour the brine and starter into the flour, and with one hand shaped like a fork, gently bring together until just combined. Once the dough starts to come together, take it out of the bowl and place on a floured work surface.

Scrape the dough off your hand into the bowl, then take out the dough and place it on your floured work surface, making sure you scrape all the dough out with a scraper to leave a clean bowl. Keep the bowl to one side, as you will need it later.

Now, with your dough on the work surface and you 'poised like a puma' (see page 18), with the heel of your hand push the dough into the work surface and 'stretch and tear', using the technique described on page 18, for about 6 minutes. Form lightly into a ball and pop back into the lightly oiled bowl you used earlier.

You now need to fold the dough, using the technique described on page 21. After folding, leave it to rest for 30 minutes, then give the dough two more folds, resting for 30 minutes each time. Between folds you will need to cover the bowl with cling film, a tea towel or a shower cap. After the final fold, leave it covered for a further 30 minutes.

MAKES I LARGE LOAF, ENOUGH FOR PLENTY OF PASTRAMI SANDWICHES

350g strong white bread flour, plus extra for dusting

100g light rye flour

60g dark rye flour

10g toasted caraway seeds

10g fine sea salt

370g pickle brine

180g rye starter (see page 33)

oil, for the bowl

150g rye flakes

YOU WILL NEED

a Dutch oven (cast-iron casserole) or a baking stone

a water spray

a baker's peel or a wooden board

Spread the rye flakes on a baking tray. Shape your dough into a long shape (see page 22) and roll it in about 200g of water. Then roll the dough in your tray of rye flakes and carpet-bomb it with the flakes to cover it completely. The water helps the rye flakes stick to the dough. Pop it seam side up in a proving basket lined with a tea towel, cover with a shower cap and pop it into the fridge overnight.

Preheat the oven to 240°C/fan 220°C/gas 9.

Once your oven is ready, put a Dutch oven (cast-iron casserole) or baking stone in to heat up for about 10 minutes. Get your water spray ready if you are using a baking stone.

If using a Dutch oven, very carefully take it out of the oven. Gently place your loaf top side down in the Dutch oven, then, using a razor blade, cut two slashes in the dough. Put the lid on, place in the oven and bake for 35 minutes, then remove the lid and bake for a further 15 minutes. Take the Dutch oven out and very carefully remove the loaf, then put it back into the oven, directly on the oven shelf, and bake for a further 5 minutes, depending on how much singe you like.

If using a baking stone, gently and slowly turn out your loaf on to a baker's peel or a wooden board, then with a sharp knife or razor blade cut two slashes in the dough. Slide it off the peel on to the baking stone in the oven, then heavily spray inside the oven with your water spray and bake for 30 minutes.

After 30 minutes, turn the loaf round and bake for a further 20 minutes, depending on how much singe you like.

Leave on a rack to cool, then enjoy with some hot salt beef and mustard – don't forget the bourbon!

BAKED CHEESECAKE

This is one of my (Matt's) top desserts. I simply love a good cheesecake and never tire of them. Perfect in my book, any time of day, with a cup of tea.

Preheat your oven to 160°C/fan 140°C/gas 3. Lightly grease a 23cm springform cake tin and line the base and sides with baking paper.

To make the sponge base, first melt the butter on a medium heat and put to one side to cool.

Using an electric mixer with the whisk attachment, whisk the eggs and sugar together until light and fluffy – this will take about 3–4 minutes on high speed. If doing it by hand, use a large bowl and a balloon whisk, roll up those sleeves and get whisking.

When the egg mix is light and fluffy, stop whisking and add the sifted flour, slowly folding it in until it is all mixed in. Pour in the warm melted butter, and again fold in slowly until everything is incorporated.

Pour the mixture into the prepared cake tin and bake for 30 minutes, or until golden brown and firm to the touch. Once baked, take it out of the oven and leave in the tin for a couple of minutes, then turn it out on to a cooling rack. Leave the oven on.

In one bowl mix together both sugars and the cornflour, and in another large bowl put the two cheeses. Slit the vanilla pods lengthways and scrape out the seeds, then add the seeds to the cheese and beat together until smooth and the seeds are all mixed through evenly. Add the sugars and cornflour to the cheese, then beat in the eggs, one at a time, making sure each one is completely mixed in before you add the next. Gradually whisk in the cream (no lumps please) and continue to whisk until thick.

Slice a 1cm thick disc off the sponge (you can freeze the rest for next time) and place the sponge disc in the bottom of the lined cake tin. Pour the cheesecake mixture over the sponge, then gently give the cake tin a wobble, just to settle the mixture.

Place the cake tin on a baking tray and bake in the oven for about 40–45 minutes, until the cake is golden brown and set. Once baked, take it out of the oven and leave it to cool for about 15 minutes before taking out of the tin.

SERVES 12

150g caster sugar

150g soft light brown sugar

16g cornflour

650g soft cream cheese

85g mascarpone cheese

2 vanilla pods

2 eggs

225g double cream

THE SPONGE BASE

60g unsalted butter, plus extra for greasing

5 eggs

150g caster sugar

150g plain flour, sifted

SALTED CHOCOLATE AND PEANUT BUTTER COOKIES

What can we say but get the kettle on? Cookies are normally soft in the middle, but these are baked through, as we prefer a crunch to our biscuits. They are absolutely delightful served with ice cream or as an ice cream sandwich.

MAKES ABOUT 60

155g peanuts

2 tablespoons demerara sugar

1 tablespoon crunchy sea salt flakes

2 vanilla pods

450g softened butter

265g caster sugar

250g demerara sugar

4 eggs

350g crunchy peanut butter

450g plain flour, sifted

2 teaspoons salt

2 teaspoons bicarbonate of soda, sifted

400g chocolate chips

Put the peanuts, the 2 tablespoons of demerara and the salt into a roasting tray and roast in the oven for 10–15 minutes, stirring every few minutes, until golden brown all over. Leave to cool.

Slit the vanilla pods lengthways, scrape out the seeds and put the seeds to one side.

In a bowl, using a wooden spoon, cream the butter, vanilla seeds and both sugars together until light and fluffy, then add the eggs one at a time. Once all is incorporated, add the rest of the ingredients and gently mix until you have a smooth but crunchy dough.

Scrape the dough out of the bowl on to a long sheet of baking paper, then roll to form a sausage shape and chill in the fridge until firm. This will take at least 2 hours, but it's best left overnight.

Preheat your oven to 160°C/fan 140°C/gas 3. Line a baking tray with baking paper. Once the dough is firm, shape into balls weighing roughly 35g each, and place on your lined baking tray. Flatten them a little – remember to leave some space between the biscuits, as they will spread out a bit. Bake in the oven for about 12 minutes if you want a soft cookie, or 16–18 minutes for a biscuit with a crunch.

Once baked, place on a cooling rack. Enjoy them warm right away, with a glass of milk, or let them cool and store them in a biscuit tin.

NORDIC BAKING

The Nordic food scene has become a global phenomenon, producing some of the world's best restaurants and chefs. Most people are bowled over when they first visit cities such as Oslo or Copenhagen – they are packed with foodie treats, and of course there are plenty of amazing bakeries too.

Unlike the southern European countries, where white bread has dominated, here the dark, dense rye rules supreme. You'll find it in everything from traditional crispbreads to the whole wheat rye breads used to make those famous open-topped sandwiches, not forgetting the beautiful cinnamon buns. With the harsh weather conditions prevalent throughout the Nordic countries, historically people would bake their bread weekly, rather than daily, so rye sourdoughs and crispbreads were perfect, as they keep for a good week or two.

Nordic breads and baking vary slightly from region to region, but also have a lot in common. Cardamom has been a staple ingredient of Nordic baking since the Vikings first encountered it during their raids on Constantinople and brought it back to the region. To this day the Nordic countries use more cardamom than anyone else in Europe, with Sweden topping the list. In this chapter you'll taste it in the Swedish rye, the cinnamon and cardamom scrolls, and even in the Finnish gingerbread cookies.

THE SWEDISH RYE

This interesting loaf always delights, with the depth and fragrance of orange, cardamom and caraway, plus the nutty crunch of the seeds on top. You want to serve this bread fresh from the oven so that everyone benefits from those aromas!

The day before you want to make your bread, make your pre-ferment. Mix the water and yeast together in a bowl, then add the flour and fully combine. Cover and leave in the fridge for 12–18 hours.

Next day, add the yeast from the day 2 list to the water and mix to dissolve. Take your pre-ferment out of the fridge – it will be nice and bubbly.

In a large bowl, mix the flours and salt together just enough for them to get to know each other, then make a well in the centre. Add the pre-ferment and the yeast and water mix to the well in the flour.

With one hand shaped like a fork, gently bring together until just combined. Scrape the dough off your hand into the bowl, then take out the dough and place on a work surface, making sure you scrape all the dough out with a scraper to leave a clean bowl.

Now, with your dough on the work surface and you 'poised like a puma' (see page 18), with the heel of your hand push the dough into the work surface and 'stretch and tear', using the technique described on page 18, for about 8 minutes. Form the dough lightly into a ball and cover with a cloth, then leave for 20 minutes to relax.

Uncover the dough and add the orange zest, cardamom and caraway seeds. 'Stretch and tear' them into the dough for a few minutes, until evenly combined, then cover with a tea towel, cling film or a shower cap and leave for 1 hour.

Line a baking tray with baking paper and sprinkle it with semolina. Divide your dough into 7 equal pieces, about 150g each, then shape each piece into a round and leave for 10 minutes.

If using, mix your seeds together, then peel and slice the onion and put to one side.

MAKES 1 LARGE LOAF, TO SERVE 4–6

DAY 1: THE PRE-FERMENT

115g cold water

2g fresh yeast

150g strong white bread flour

DAY 2

6g fresh yeast

300g water

300g strong white bread flour

170g rye flour

10g fine sea salt

zest of 1 orange

4g ground cardamom

5g caraway seeds

semolina, for the tray

optional: sunflower, pumpkin and fennel seeds, for sprinkling

optional: 1 small onion

YOU WILL NEED

a water spray

Roll your rested dough pieces into smooth tight buns (see page 25). Place them on the baking tray with one in the centre and the other six round it. Brush them all over with water, and then the next stage is up to you. You can sprinkle seeds all over them, or leave them plain – but what we like to do is sprinkle one with seeds, then one with a sliced onion, and so on.

Cover with a tea towel and leave to prove for 45 minutes, until they are looking very proud and saying to you, 'I am ready for the oven.'

While the loaf is proving, preheat your oven to 250°C/fan 230°C/gas 10 or as hot as it will go. Get your water spray ready.

Once proved, put the baking tray into the oven and spray inside the oven with your water spray. Bake for 20 minutes, then turn the tray round and bake for a further 10–15 minutes, until the bread is golden brown.

Allow to cool a little, then place in the middle of your table and enjoy!

THE NUT LOAF

This amazing loaf comes from Denmark and is a firm favourite at Bread Ahead. It isn't really 'bread', as no flour is used, but please don't think it's destined for the bird table, as it is absolutely delicious. The ingredients mean it is fairly expensive to make, but it's worth every penny, and is so easy to prepare and bake. This loaf is really just delicious on its own, but very cheeky with some chocolate spread!

MAKES I SMALL LOAF –
THINLY SLICED,
WILL FEED 4–6

50g hazelnuts

50g almonds

50g sesame seeds

50g buckwheat

125g sunflower seeds

125g pumpkin seeds

100g walnuts

25g linseeds

25g dill or fennel seeds

50g poppy seeds

4g fine sea salt

85g rapeseed oil

5 eggs

a good few twists (6–8)
of black pepper

Preheat the oven to 180°C/fan 160°C/gas 4, and roast the hazelnuts, almonds, sesame seeds and buckwheat. You can do them all together in a baking tray or roast them separately, depending on how much of that 'roasted' flavour you like. We like an adult roasting, so fairly dark. Start with about 10 minutes, then give them a stir and put back into the oven to finish off. You can also do the roasting on the hob, using a large frying pan and continually tossing until you have got a good even colour on them. Once roasted, leave to cool.

When cool, place all the 10 types of grain, seeds and nuts in a large bowl and stir in the salt. Add the oil and eggs and mix thoroughly. Cover the bowl and leave to rest for 30 minutes.

Preheat your oven to 160°C/fan 140°C/gas 3.

Uncover the bowl and stir the mixture, then pour into a loaf tin 18cm x 8cm x 6cm and smooth the top with the back of a spoon. Bake in the centre of the oven for 50 minutes.

Once baked, turn the loaf out of the tin and place on a rack to cool.

Serve thinly sliced, with butter or on its own – or with a bit of chocolate spread.

RYE CRISPBREADS

These crispbreads have a great tang to them and keep really well. It's always good to have your biscuit tin filled up with these – they are perfect with cheese, or just to munch on their own as a snack. We have a special rolling pin for knocking the classic dimples in, but you can just fork them over.

MAKES 4 LARGE CRISPBREADS

200g wholegrain rye flour

½ teaspoon fine sea salt

1 teaspoon caster sugar

40g rye starter (see page 33)

100g water

optional: crunchy coarse sea salt

YOU WILL NEED

a water spray

Preheat your oven to 200°C/fan 180°C/gas 6 and line a couple of baking trays with baking paper.

Put the rye flour, salt and sugar into a bowl and mix them together just enough for them to get to know each other. Make a well in the centre.

In another bowl, mix the starter with the water. Once fully combined, pour the liquid into the well in the flour. With your hand shaped like a fork, bring the ingredients together to form a stiff dough. If required, you can move the dough to a work surface and 'stretch and tear' briefly, using the technique described on page 18, to ensure that the ingredients are fully combined. Cover the dough with a tea towel, cling film or a shower cap and leave to rest for 20 minutes.

Now divide the dough into 4 equal pieces and shape them into loose rounds. Using a rolling pin, roll each piece out as thinly as you can (no more than 2mm thick). You can roll them to whatever shape you like, from round to rectangle, and you can also cut them out with a pastry cutter, to make small crackers.

If you have a dimpled rolling pin, roll it over the crackers to put those classic dimples in, but otherwise you can simply use a fork to fork them over. Spray them with water and sprinkle them with coarse sea salt, if you like.

Place your crackers on the prepared baking trays. Bake for 6 minutes, then turn them over and bake for a further 6–8 minutes, until crisp and brown all over. Smaller crackers, once turned over, will need only a further 4 minutes.

Allow them to cool, then enjoy. They will keep well in an airtight tin for 3 weeks, if not longer.

CINNAMON AND CARDAMOM SCROLLS

These buns! Sticky, buttery, and with a heady aroma of cinnamon and cardamom, they are hard to resist, and are the perfect excuse to justify elevenses. I (Louise) was always being asked for these bad boys in our Nordic Baking class, so here they are!

To make the dough, put the milk, sugar, yeast, salt, ground and crushed cardamom, melted butter and egg, plus yolk, into a large bowl and whisk together for just 30 seconds. Gradually add the flour and mix with one hand until it is all incorporated into a dough.

Scrape the dough off your hand back into the bowl, then scrape the fairly sticky dough out of the bowl on to a floured work surface. Make sure you scrape all the dough out with a scraper to leave a clean bowl, keeping the bowl, as you will need it later.

Now, with your dough on the work surface and you 'poised like a puma' (see page 18), with the heel of your hand push the dough into the work surface and 'stretch and tear', using the technique described on page 18, for about 6 minutes. Form lightly into a ball and cover with a cloth, then leave for 10 minutes to relax.

Rub all over the inside of the bowl you used earlier with the olive oil, then, when the 10 minutes are up, reshape the dough into a round and place it in the centre of the bowl.

You now need to fold the dough, using the technique described on page 21. After folding, leave it to rest for 30 minutes, then give the dough two more folds, resting for 30 minutes each time. Between folds you will need to cover the bowl with cling film, a tea towel or a shower cap. After the final fold, put it into the fridge for 30 minutes – this will just firm up the dough ready for rolling out.

To make the filling, beat the softened butter, sugars and cinnamon together in a bowl until combined.

Take the dough out of the fridge after its final rest and transfer it on to a lightly floured work surface. Using a rolling pin, roll it out into a rectangle about 50cm x 40cm. Spread the filling evenly over the dough, leaving a small strip clear of any filling along one of the long edges, then brush this strip with

MAKES 12

300g full fat milk

80g caster sugar

10g fresh yeast

2g fine sea salt

3 teaspoons ground cardamom

1 teaspoon cardamom seeds, crushed

100g unsalted butter, melted

1 egg

1 egg yolk

450g plain flour, plus extra for dusting

50g rye flour

olive oil, for the bowl

THE FILLING

180g softened unsalted butter

225g soft dark brown sugar

75g soft light brown sugar

20g ground cinnamon

THE STICKY GLAZE

200g caster sugar

juice of 1 lemon

juice of 1 orange

1 cinnamon stick

a little water (this strip will be used to seal the dough once it's rolled).

Roll up the dough lengthways, gently pressing the filling-free edge into the dough to seal it.

Line a baking tray with baking paper, then cut the roll into 12 pieces about 5cm thick. Carefully transfer them to the prepared baking tray, then gently press them down by about 1cm, so they are about 4cm high, and cover with a tea towel. Leave to prove in a warm place for about 1 hour, until almost doubled in size and touching each other.

Preheat your oven to 200°C/fan 180°C/gas 6.

Bake the proved buns for 15 minutes, then turn the tray round and bake for a further 10 minutes, until golden brown.

To make the syrup for glazing the buns, just place all the glaze ingredients in a small saucepan. Heat on a low heat, just enough to dissolve the sugar, then turn the heat up to boiling. Lower the heat again and simmer fast for a couple of minutes, then take off the heat. You don't have to make the glaze, but it does add a real sweet decadence to the buns.

Once baked, remove the buns from the oven and transfer them on to a wire rack, but leave them in the tray while you glaze them (so the sugary caramel gets absorbed into the buns). Brush the glaze generously over them, then eat warm, maybe with a nice dollop of cold whipped cream!

TOSCAKAKA (TOSCA ALMOND CAKE)

This double-layered cake, with a lovely light buttery sponge on the bottom and a crunchy crisp almondy top, is a real delight to bake, and of course to eat too. Try it with some fresh blackberries and cream, or even turn it into a Victoria sandwich, with raspberry jam sandwiched in the middle.

MAKES 1 CAKE –
SERVES 8–12

THE CAKE

180g unsalted butter

180g caster sugar

3 eggs

1 egg yolk

180g self-raising flour, sifted

2 teaspoons almond extract

THE TOPPING

200g salted butter

50g honey

150g caster sugar

50g soft light brown sugar

60g full fat milk

40g plain flour, sifted

50g ground almonds

200g flaked almonds

Preheat your oven to 180°C/fan 160°C/gas 4.

Lightly grease a 26cm springform cake tin and line the base and sides with baking paper.

Make the topping first. Melt the butter, honey and sugars together in a medium saucepan on a low heat, then stir in the milk, flour, ground almonds and flaked almonds, and put to one side.

To make the cake, first cream the butter and sugar together until light and fluffy, either using a mixer with a beater attachment, or in a bowl with a wooden spoon. Beat the eggs and yolk together in a small jug or bowl, then very slowly add them to the creamed butter and sugar, whisking all the time to prevent splitting. Fold in the flour and almond extract until it is all incorporated.

Pour into the prepared cake tin, then smooth the mixture out to the sides of the tin and level the top with the back of a spoon. Bake for 18 minutes, then remove the cake from the oven and increase the oven temperature to 200°C/fan 180°C/gas 6. Gently and evenly spoon the topping mix over the cake, then put back into the oven for 20 minutes, until golden brown and a skewer comes out clean.

Take out of the oven and cool in the tin for 20 minutes, then unclip to release the cake. Either serve warm immediately, or leave on a rack to cool completely.

PIPARKAKUT

These Finnish spiced biscuits have a lovely sharp and warming flavour, and are normally baked for a Christmas treat. This recipe makes enough dough to fill your biscuit tin to overflowing, perfect for presents over the festive holidays.

Put the honey, black treacle, butter and sugar into a saucepan, then place on a low heat and melt all the ingredients together. Once melted, leave to cool for 20 minutes (make sure the butter is completely cool – don't use it warm).

Sift the flour, bicarbonate of soda and all the spices into a large mixing bowl and give them a mix.

Pour the treacle mix into the flour mix. Crack in the eggs and add the orange zest, then, with a heavy hand (as this mix is fairly stiff), stir all the ingredients together and mix well until all is evenly combined and a smooth dark paste is formed.

Shape the dough into a ball and pop it back into the bowl, then cover and pop it into the fridge for 3–4 hours to rest and firm up.

Take out of the fridge and leave to soften for about 1 hour.

Preheat your oven to 160°C/fan 140°C/gas 3 and line a baking tray with baking paper.

On a lightly floured work surface, roll your dough out nice and thin, to just a couple of millimetres thick. Cut your biscuits out to any shape you like, then place them on the lined baking tray and bake for 14 minutes.

Once baked, let them cool on the tray.

MAKES ABOUT 50

100g pure honey

120g black treacle

270g unsalted butter

180g soft dark brown sugar

680g plain flour, plus extra for dusting

2 teaspoons bicarbonate of soda

20g ground cinnamon

10g ground cloves

10g ground cardamom

24g ground ginger

6g ground mace

6g ground allspice

2 eggs

zest of 2 oranges

EASTERN EUROPEAN BAKING

At Bread Ahead, since we opened our doors in 2013, we have been very lucky in having bakers of many different nationalities working here. They come from all around the world, but especially from Eastern European countries like Poland, Romania, Hungary and Slovakia.

We have learnt so much from those bakers and their grandmothers over the years, with them bringing in stories and family recipes for us to try, and have had many heated discussions in the bakery about whose mother's recipe is the best (we normally sit on the fence for this one).

There is huge diversity within this region, but many similarities too. Lots of their rye breads are sweetened with sugar, molasses and honey, and are also spiced with caraway and coriander, like the Borodinsky rye bread. White bread is also often sweetened and topped with poppy seeds.

In Eastern Europe, people love to honour religious festivals with celebratory enriched breads, the most famous being the Easter breads like the paska. The name changes from area to area but you will find them in many countries, often moulded into elaborate shapes, plaits and religious symbols.

In most Eastern European countries, it is customary to present honoured guests with a loaf of bread, which is something we could all learn from!

BORODINSKY RYE

This Russian rye bread has a great story behind it, as Louise loves to tell every class that gets to make the loaf. The legend goes that after the Battle of Borodino, nuns at a convent established by a widow of the Napoleonic Wars started making this loaf, with the round coriander seeds representing the shots fired on the battlefield.

Whatever its origins, this bread is absolutely packed with flavour and will happily keep in your bread bin for a week. A good tip is to bake it the day before you need it – it is easier to slice once it has had a day to settle. It's exactly what we do in the bakery.

Feed your starter a good 8 hours before you make the pre-ferment, so it is nice and lively. The day before you want to make your bread, make the pre-ferment. Mix the starter and water together in a bowl, add the flour and bring together to form a nice loose mixture. Cover and leave at room temperature for 12–24 hours.

When you're ready to start making the bread, uncover your pre-ferment. It should have lots of air bubbles in it and have a pleasant, slightly alcoholic aroma. Put all the day 2 ingredients into a bowl along with the pre-ferment. With your hand shaped like a fork, bring the mixture together and continue mixing for a good 2 minutes until fully combined, then cover and leave to rest for 10 minutes.

Lightly oil an 18cm x 8cm x 6cm loaf tin, and line it with baking paper. Heavily dust your work surface with rye flour, then tip your dough on to it. Roll it in the flour, then place in the prepared tin and dust the top with more rye flour.

Leave to rise for 2–3 hours (the flour on the surface of the bread will start to crack when it's ready).

Preheat the oven to 230°C/fan 210°C/gas 8. Get your water spray ready. When your bread has risen, place it in the oven and spray inside the oven with your water spray. Bake for 40 minutes, then pop the loaf out of the tin and put it back into the oven, directly on the oven shelf, and bake for a further 5 minutes.

Take the bread out of the oven and place on a cooling rack. Allow to cool for a good 2 hours, but it's best to leave it overnight before you slice and eat. Ridiculously delicious served thinly sliced with salted butter or cold meats and fish.

MAKES I SMALL LOAF, BUT SLICED THINLY IT GOES A LONG WAY, AS IT IS PACKED WITH FLAVOUR

DAY I: THE PRE-FERMENT

75g rye starter (see page 33)

140g cold water

100g rye flour

DAY 2

175g rye flour, plus extra for dusting

6g fine sea salt

10g caraway seeds

10g coriander seeds

1 teaspoon molasses

130g cold water

oil, for the tin

YOU WILL NEED

a water spray

CINNAMON STRUDEL BABKAS

This is one of the stars of the show in our Eastern European baking workshop. 'Babka' means 'grandmother', and this is a traditional Eastern European cake with many variations. We're not sure if our version is more of a bread or a cake, but either way it's delicious!

MAKES 12

THE DOUGH

450g strong white bread flour, plus extra for dusting

4g fine sea salt

10g caster sugar

5g ground nutmeg

280g milk

50g butter

8g fresh yeast

THE FILLING

30g ground cinnamon

75g caster sugar

75g soft dark brown sugar

150g butter

1 egg, beaten, for the eggwash

Put the flour, salt, sugar and nutmeg for the dough into a bowl and combine, just enough for them to get to know each other. Make a well in the centre of the flour.

Measure the milk and butter into a small saucepan and heat until the butter starts to soften (important: do not let the temperature go above 30°C).

Remove from the heat, add the yeast, and mix until dissolved (if using instant/quick/fast-acting dried yeast, mix the yeast through the dry flour mixture instead). Pour the liquid into the well in the flour, and with one hand gently bring the dough together. Once it starts coming together, take it out of the bowl and place it on your work surface. Don't add any flour.

Now, with your dough on the work surface and you 'poised like a puma' (see page 18), with the heel of your hand push the dough into the work surface and 'stretch and tear' for 8 minutes, using the technique described on page 18. Your dough will become nice and elasticated and have a velvety feel. Put it back into the bowl, then cover and leave at room temperature for 1 hour.

To make the filling, mix the cinnamon and sugars together in a small bowl, then mix in the butter until combined.

Roll out the dough on a lightly floured surface to form a rectangle about 40cm x 30cm. Spread the filling evenly over the dough, leaving a small strip clear of filling along one of the long edges (this strip will be used to seal the dough once it's rolled), then brush the clear strip with the eggwash.

Roll up the dough lengthways, gently pressing the filling-free edge into the dough to seal it.

Line a baking tray with baking paper, then cut the roll into 12 pieces and place them cut side up on the tray. Gently open each babka up with your fingers, then leave to rise at room temperature for 1 hour, until risen and touching each other.

To make the strudel topping, mix the flour and sugars together in a bowl, then rub in the butter. Once rubbed in and looking like coarse sand, pop the topping into the fridge while the babkas are rising.

Preheat your oven to 220°C/fan 200°C/gas 7. Get your water spray ready.

Dollop a teaspoonful of jam in the centre of each babka, and sprinkle with the strudel topping. Place in the oven and lightly spray inside the oven with your water spray. Bake for 20 minutes, then turn the tray round and bake for a further 10 minutes more.

Leave to cool a little, then enjoy warm, with extra-thick double cream.

THE STRUDEL TOPPING

75g flour

75g sugar

15g demerara sugar

45g butter

a pinch of fine sea salt

raspberry jam

YOU WILL NEED

a water spray

KOLACE

These little buttery puffed-up pieces of yeasted dough, from the Czech/Slovak region, are a delight. 'Kolace' means 'circle', and they hold various fillings like cream cheese, jam, bacon or poppy seeds. Traditionally these are served in their hundreds on large platters at weddings, with several different fillings, so they look really colourful.

We love to bake them for lunch, especially the bacon ones, which we sometimes top with grated cheese as well.

MAKES 12

15g fresh yeast

250g full fat milk

2 large eggs

80g caster sugar

6g fine sea salt

zest of 1 lemon

3g ground mace

550g strong white bead flour, plus extra for dusting

125g softened unsalted butter

1 egg, beaten, for the eggwash

YOU WILL NEED

a 9cm pastry cutter

In a bowl, dissolve the yeast in the milk. Put the eggs, sugar, salt, lemon zest, mace and flour into another large bowl and add the yeast mixture.

With one hand shaped like a fork, gently bring together until just combined. Scrape the dough off your hand into the bowl, then take the dough out of the bowl and place on a work surface, making sure you scrape all the dough out with a scraper to leave a clean bowl. Keep the bowl to one side, as you will need it later.

Now, with your dough on the work surface and you 'poised like a puma' (see page 18), with the heel of your hand push the dough into the work surface and 'stretch and tear', using the technique described on page 18, for about 5 minutes. Cover and leave to rest for 10 minutes.

Return your dough to the work surface. Cut the butter into quarters, then, one at a time, break each quarter down into little pieces and place these on the dough. Again 'poised like a puma', with the heel of your hand push the dough into the work surface and 'stretch and tear' to incorporate the butter. This should take about 1½ minutes per quarter. Make sure you scrape your dough to the centre throughout, so that the butter is mixed through evenly. Once all the butter has been incorporated, the dough should be glossy, smooth and elastic when pulled.

Form the dough into a ball, dust the inside of the bowl you used earlier with flour, then pop the dough back into the bowl and cover with cling film. Leave until it has doubled in size (this will take about 1–2 hours).

Lightly grease a large baking tray, or line it with baking paper. Roll out the dough on your work surface to about 1cm thick, then, using a 9cm pastry cutter, cut out circles and place them on the baking tray. Re-roll any scraps and cut out again. Leave to prove for about 2 hours, until the height has doubled.

Preheat your oven to 180°C/fan 160°C/gas 4.

Using your thumb or the back of a spoon, press 1 large or 2 smaller deep indentations into the centre of each dough circle, leaving a wide rim. Brush the edges with the eggwash. Spoon roughly 1 tablespoon of your desired filling into the indentation. If using white sauce, lay some smoked salmon over the top or sprinkle with bacon lardons. If using the cream cheese filling, just sprinkle poppy seeds over the top.

Bake for about 10 minutes for jam, stewed apple and lemon curd, and a further 2 minutes for the smoked salmon, bacon and cream cheese ones.

Transfer to a rack and leave to cool.

FILLINGS

jam

stewed apple with cinnamon

lemon curd

cream cheese and poppy seeds

Mrs G's white sauce (see page 147) and fried smoked bacon lardons or smoked salmon

BLACK RUSSIAN BAGELS

We ate these for the first time in a tiny market about an hour's drive from the outskirts of Moscow – they were filled with smoked fish and fish eggs, sandwiched together with sour cream . . . wow! They are delicious, especially with a few chilled vodkas.

MAKES 12

DAY 1: THE POOLISH
(SEE PAGE 15)

2g fresh yeast

50g water

50g rye flour

DAY 2

265g water

5g fresh yeast

220g strong white bread flour, plus extra for dusting

120g rye flour

140g whole wheat flour

100g black treacle

25g cocoa powder

10g fine sea salt

1 teaspoon caraway seeds

60g caster sugar

oil, for greasing

egg white, for brushing

TOPPINGS

crunchy sea salt, poppy seeds, sesame seeds, onion flakes, garlic flakes

On day 1, make the poolish. Mix the yeast with the water until dissolved, then stir in the rye flour until a thick paste is formed. Cover and place in the fridge overnight.

Next day (day 2), put the water into a large bowl and mix in your poolish, which will be nice and bubbly by now. Add the yeast, flours, treacle, cocoa, salt and seeds, then, with one hand shaped like a fork, gently bring together until just combined. Scrape the dough off your hand into the bowl, then take the dough out of the bowl and place on a work surface, making sure you scrape all the dough out with a scraper to leave a clean bowl.

Now, with your dough on the work surface and you 'poised like a puma' (see page 18), with the heel of your hand push the dough into the work surface and 'stretch and tear' for about 4 minutes, using the technique described on page 18. Cover and leave to rest for 2 hours.

Once your dough has rested, divide it into 12 pieces (about 80g each) and shape them into loose balls. Cover and leave to relax for 10 minutes.

Preheat your oven to 240°C/fan 220°C/gas 9. Roll out the pieces of dough to 20–25cm long and shape them into bagels (see page 170). Place them on a floured tray, cover and leave to prove for 30 minutes. Meanwhile, put the sugar into a large heavy-based saucepan with 4 litres of water. Bring to the boil, then reduce to a simmer. Line two baking trays with oiled baking paper.

Poaching time: gently lift up each bagel and pop into the simmering water. Don't crowd the saucepan, do it in batches. Poach your bagels for approximately 20 seconds on each side, total 40 seconds, then place them on the lined baking trays, spacing them out evenly.

Brush them with egg white, then sprinkle with sea salt flakes and the rest of your toppings. Bake for 15 minutes, until the toppings are all crispy. These make the perfect smoked salmon bagels.

PASKA

Paska is an enriched sweet bread, not a million miles away from a brioche. It is traditionally enjoyed at Easter time in the Ukraine and in Russia.

The day before you want to bake your bread, put the milk and yeast into a large bowl, stir to dissolve the yeast, then whisk in the egg.

Add the flour, orange zest, salt and sugar to the bowl, then, with one hand shaped like a fork, gently bring together until just combined. Scrape the dough off your hand into the bowl, then take the dough out of the bowl and place on a work surface, making sure you scrape all the dough out with a scraper to leave a clean bowl. Keep the bowl to one side, as you will need it later.

Now, with your dough on the work surface and you 'poised like a puma' (see page 18), with the heel of your hand push the dough into the work surface and 'stretch and tear', using the technique described on page 18, for about 6 minutes. Form into a ball, then cover and leave to rest for 5 minutes.

Again 'poised like a puma', with the heel of your hand push the dough into the work surface and 'stretch and tear' to incorporate the butter a little at a time – this should take about 2–3 minutes. Make sure you scrape your dough to the centre throughout the 'stretching and tearing', to make sure the butter is mixed through evenly. When the butter has all been incorporated, the dough should be glossy, smooth and elastic when pulled.

Form the dough into a ball, dust the inside of the bowl you used earlier with flour, then pop the dough back into the bowl. Cover with cling film and leave until it has doubled in size (this will take about 1–2 hours), then put into the fridge overnight to chill.

MAKES 1 LARGE LOAF,
TO SERVE 8–10

350g full fat milk

10g fresh yeast

1 egg

650g strong white bread flour, plus extra for dusting

zest of 1 orange

10g salt

25g caster sugar

80g softened butter

1 egg white, beaten, for brushing

1 egg, beaten, for the eggwash

Next day, divide the dough into 2 pieces, one weighing 850g and one weighing 300g, and form them both into rounds. Cover and leave for 10 minutes.

Now roll the larger piece of dough into a tight ball and place it in a 20cm round bread tin lined with baking paper. Flatten it down a wee bit. Brush the top of the dough with beaten egg white.

Divide the other (300g) piece of dough into 3 equal pieces. Roll them into 60cm lengths and plait them together.

Either place your plait round the edge of the larger piece of dough, or use it to form a cross over the top. Cover the dough and leave it to prove for about 2½–3 hours, until doubled in size.

Preheat your oven to 180°C/fan 160°C/gas 4.

Gently brush all over the top of the dough with eggwash and bake for 35 minutes, until the paska is golden brown and looking magnificent.

Once baked, enjoy warm.

PIEKARZ KANAPKA – 'THE BAKER'S SANDWICH'

These have been made by many of our Polish bakers over the last few years. They're a real treat for breakfast, especially if you have a few people to feed. Allow two buns per person.

MAKES 22 BUNS

560g strong white bread flour, plus extra for dusting

10g fine sea salt

50g caster sugar

12g fresh yeast

190g full fat milk

3 eggs

65g softened unsalted butter

slices of salty ham and a good strong melting cheese, such as Koldamer

sea salt and cracked black pepper

1 egg, beaten, for the eggwash

1 tablespoon poppy seeds

These are best prepared the day before and baked fresh for breakfast the next morning.

Line a baking tray with baking paper. Measure the flour, salt and sugar into a bowl and combine. Make a well in the centre of the flour.

In another bowl, add the yeast to the milk and stir until dissolved, then whisk in the eggs. Pour the liquid into the well in the flour, then gently bring the dough together. Once it starts to come together, take it out of the bowl and place it on a work surface (don't add any extra flour).

Now, with the dough on the work surface and you 'poised like a puma' (see page 18), with the heel of your hand push the dough into the work surface and 'stretch and tear', using the technique described on page 18, for 6–8 minutes. Shape into a ball, pop it back into the bowl, sprinkle the dough with a little flour, then cover and let it rest for 10 minutes.

Return your dough to the work surface, then slowly add the butter to the dough, a little at a time, as you continue to 'stretch and tear' to incorporate the butter. Continue until all the butter is incorporated, being careful not to add it too quickly (add about 15g at a time).

Once the butter is incorporated, continue to 'stretch and tear' for 1 minute, then again form into a ball. Pop it back into the bowl, then cover and let it rest for another 10 minutes.

Divide the dough into 40g pieces and roll them into tight smooth balls. Place them on the prepared tray and pop them into the fridge for 20 minutes to firm up. The next step is quite unusual – making up a sandwich but using raw dough!

Take your dough balls out of the fridge and slice them in half horizontally, using a very sharp knife. Remove the tops and pile in the ham and cheese with a good sprinkling of salt and black pepper. Pop the tops back on, squeeze them back on to the lined baking tray so that they are nearly touching, then generously brush with the eggwash and carpet-bomb them with poppy seeds.

Leave to prove until they are all kissing and touching each other (about 1 hour), then cover loosely with cling film and pop into the fridge overnight.

Next day, take them out of the fridge and leave for about 1 hour, to come up to room temperature.

Preheat your oven to 200°C/fan 180°C/gas 6.

Remove the cling film from the buns and pop them into the oven for 18 minutes, until golden brown.

Eat while hot – these are great for breakfast, and amazing as a late-night snack with friends.

ORESHKI (WALNUT BISCUITS)

To do these properly you will need an oreshki mould. They are easy to buy online, and you can get a stovetop one or an electric one. 'Oreshki' means 'walnut', and these biscuits resemble those nuts. Traditionally they are filled with caramel.

MAKES 100 SHELLS –
50 FILLED DELIGHTS

150g butter

2 eggs

1 teaspoon vanilla extract

4g fine sea salt

2 tablespoons sugar

5g baking powder

335g plain flour, sifted

YOU WILL NEED
an oreshki mould
(see above)

Melt the butter on a low heat and leave to cool. Once cool, pour it into a large bowl and whisk in the eggs and vanilla. Now add the salt, sugar, baking powder and flour and mix together until a dough is formed.

Roll the dough into 5–6g balls and pop them on a baking tray lined with baking paper.

Preheat your oreshki mould until it's nice and hot, then place the balls in the mould. Don't worry about pressing them down, the dough will spread when you're squeezing the two sides of the mould together. Cook on the hob for about 3–5 minutes on each side or until golden – you can check by just opening the mould and having a look. Once baked on both sides, carefully remove from the mould and leave to cool.

Using a very sharp knife, cut each of the walnut-shaped cookies out by trimming the edges, so each shell is perfect.

Spoon your desired filling (see ideas below) into the shells and sandwich them together in pairs to form the 'walnuts'.

CHOCOLATE AND CARAMEL FILLING

310g caster sugar

300g dark chocolate (70%), chopped up, or buttons

375g double cream

Put the sugar into a pan and melt over a medium heat, stirring occasionally, until it becomes a dark brown caramel. Take off the heat and stir in the chocolate, then add the cream and return to the heat. Heat slowly until a smooth sauce is formed, then pour through a sieve into a container and chill in the fridge until it has firmed up.

CARAMEL FILLING

2 x 397g tins of condensed milk

Put the unopened tins into a large saucepan and cover with water. Bring the water to the boil, then simmer gently for 3 hours, topping up the water so that the tins always remain completely covered.

Remove the tins from the water and leave to cool completely before you open them.

GREAT BRITISH BAKING

Nothing to do with a certain television show, this chapter is full of recipes from Scotland, Wales and Ireland.

You mustn't just think of deep-fried Mars bars, leeks and Guinness! These regions of Great Britain are all rich in natural resources in their own unique way, and have countless traditional recipes that have been handed down for generations, to make the most of what is readily available locally. Many of these recipes date from times when people were mostly cooking on open fires, using flat griddles or bakestones, like the Welsh cakes and the potato farls. Justin's own family recipe in this chapter, Gellatly's bannock, is still made on an open fire.

People have fiercely guarded and retained many of the ancient and classic traditions, and this is true of their cuisine and baking as well. Of course, within these countries and regions every family has its own take on the traditional classics. Differences range from variations in ingredients, to how they are baked, and even which way you stir the mix!

Ultimately, all the recipes in this chapter, from bara brith, the beautiful fruit and tea loaf from Wales, to traditional Irish soda bread, are unfussy, simple and very tasty. Most of all, they will keep the fire burning in your belly all day (especially those Aberdeen butteries).

ABERDEEN BUTTERIES

Aberdeen butteries or rowies are a classic Scottish breakfast roll, typically served with jam. They are every bit as indulgent as croissants but much easier to make.

DAY 1: THE PRE-FERMENT Put the yeast and 25g of the water into a small bowl and stir to dissolve the yeast, then stir in the sugar. Cover and leave for about 1 hour to get lively. For a richer flavour in your dough, you can make your pre-ferment the night before and place it in the fridge overnight.

DAY 2: Place the flour and salt in a large bowl and mix together just enough for them to get to know each other. Make a well in the centre, then add the pre-ferment and the rest of the water (145g).

With one hand shaped like a fork, gently bring together until just combined. Scrape the dough off your hand into the bowl, then take the dough out of the bowl and place on a work surface, making sure you scrape all the dough out with a scraper to leave a clean bowl. Keep the bowl to one side, as you will need it later.

Now, with your dough on the work surface and you 'poised like a puma' (see page 18), with the heel of your hand push the dough into the work surface and 'stretch and tear', using the technique described on page 18, for about 8 minutes, making sure you scrape your dough to the centre throughout the 'stretching and tearing', to make sure the dough develops evenly.

Lightly flour the inside of the bowl you used earlier, then form your dough into a round and put it back into the bowl. Cover with a tea towel, cling film or a shower cap and leave for 20 minutes at room temperature.

In a separate bowl, mix the butter and lard together until well combined. Place your dough on a floured surface and, using a rolling pin, roll it out into a rectangle about 40cm x 20cm. Spread half of the butter mixture over half the dough, then fold the uncovered half over the buttered side. Roll the dough out into a rectangle again, spread the remainder of the butter mixture over half the dough, then fold it over again.

MAKES 8 CRISPY,
BUTTERY DELIGHTS

10g fresh yeast (or 5g instant/quick/fast-acting dried yeast)

170g warm water

10g soft light brown sugar

250g strong white bread flour, plus extra for dusting

5g salt

125g unsalted butter

70g lard

crunchy sea salt flakes

You will need to repeat the fold twice more, resting the dough in the fridge for 20 minutes each time. Once finished, wrap it in cling film and leave to rest in the fridge for 30 minutes.

Take your dough out of the fridge and cut it into 8 equal pieces. Using your fingers, form them into roughly round shapes and leave to rise for about 1 hour, until puffed up. Sprinkle them with crunchy sea salt.

Preheat your oven to 220°C/fan 200°C/gas 7, and bake the rolls for 25 minutes, until very crisp and golden brown.

Take them out of the oven (watch out – the tray will have hot melted butter in it), and serve warm.

BARA BRITH

This sweet loaf comes from Wales, and is generally eaten at teatime. We really enjoy it with a slice or two of the famous Gorwydd Caerphilly and a crisp pear, or more simply with lashings of butter and a mug of tea.

MAKES ABOUT 10 SLICES

180ml strong hot tea, such as Earl Grey, Darjeeling or builders', but you can add a smoky background with some lapsang souchong if you like

40g fragrant pure honey, plus extra for glazing

100g currants

50g raisins

50g sultanas

50g chopped prunes

butter, for greasing

230g self-raising flour

1 teaspoon ground mixed spice

a pinch of fine sea salt

zest of 1 lemon

60g caster sugar

60g demerara sugar

1 egg, beaten

45g full fat milk

The day before you want to make this loaf you need to soak your fruit, so make your tea in a large bowl (and don't forget to make yourself a cup too). Add the honey, currants, raisins, sultanas and chopped prunes, mix well, then cover with cling film and leave overnight.

Next day, preheat your oven to 160°C/fan 140°C/gas 3. Grease a 20cm x 10cm x 6cm loaf tin and line it with baking paper.

Uncover your soaked fruit – you will find that most of the tea has been absorbed, leaving juicy plump fruit. Sift the flour and mixed spice on top of the fruit, then add the salt, lemon zest, sugars, beaten egg and milk, and mix together until all incorporated evenly. Spoon into the prepared loaf tin and level the top with the back of a spoon.

Bake in the preheated oven for 55 minutes – the bara brith will be ready when it's golden brown and firm to the touch, and a skewer comes out clean.

Take out of the oven and brush with honey, then leave to cool in the tin for 5 minutes before turning out. All you need now is a generous amount of salted butter and some Gorwydd Caerphilly.

POTATO FARL

This quick and simple Irish potato bread is the star of the famous Irish breakfast and makes a great accompaniment to many meals, Irish or otherwise.

If cooking in the oven (as opposed to on the hob), preheat it to 200°C/fan 180°C/gas 6.

Mash the potatoes with the melted butter and season to taste (we go quite heavy on the seasoning). Add the flour, baking powder, red onion and spring onions and mix together until well incorporated.

Push your potato dough down to form a disc about 12cm across, then cut the disc into 4 pieces. Place them in a hot, dry ovenproof pan (no oil or butter) for 4 minutes, then carefully turn them over and cook for an additional 4 minutes – you can do this on the hob or in the oven. (If cooking on the hob, be careful they don't burn).

Take out of the pan or oven and serve with your fry-up!

MAKES 4

125g boiled potatoes (made with about 200g potatoes such as Maris Piper)

15g unsalted butter, melted

fine sea salt and ground white pepper, to taste

50g plain flour

½ teaspoon baking powder

2 tablespoons sliced red onion (about 1 small onion)

2 spring onions, finely sliced (including the green stalks)

SODA BREAD

This traditional Irish bread is one of the simplest and quickest to make in the book, with no yeast, a quick mix by hand and a pretty short resting time. The cross on top was originally made to ward off the devil and protect the household, or even to release the devil from the loaf. Whatever the story behind it, it's a great loaf of bread.

Preheat your oven to 200°C/fan 180°C/gas 6 and line a baking tray with baking paper.

In a large bowl mix all the dry ingredients together just enough for them to get to know each other. Pour in the black treacle, buttermilk and water, then mix together until a wet sticky dough is formed.

Rub your hands with some flour (like a gymnast), then bring the dough together to form into a ball and place on the prepared baking tray.

Rub the oil all over the top of the dough and sprinkle heavily with coarse oatmeal. Cut a cross through the dough about a quarter of the way through, using a serrated knife, and leave to rest for 8 minutes. Then bake in the preheated oven for 40 minutes, until bloomed out like a flower and golden brown.

Take out of the oven and place on a rack to cool.

MAKES 1 MEDIUM LOAF,
ENOUGH TO SERVE 4–6

250g coarse wholemeal flour

250g self-raising flour, plus extra for dusting

80g coarse oatmeal, plus extra for dusting

6g bicarbonate of soda

12g fine sea salt

25g black treacle

250g buttermilk

200g water

1 teaspoon olive oil

SCOTTISH SHORTBREAD

Buttery, short and crisp – a delight for any biscuit tin!

Preheat your oven to 120°C/fan 100°C/gas ½ and line a baking tray with baking paper.

Sift the flour into a large bowl and add the diced cold butter. Rub the butter into the flour until the mixture looks like breadcrumbs, then add the sugars and salt and continue to mix until a crumbly but smooth paste is reached.

You can rest this dough after it's made, but it's easier to roll it out straight away. Roll it out to form a 30cm square about 4mm thick, then cut out shapes using a 6cm round pastry cutter. Bring the trimmings together and re-roll, then place all the biscuits on your prepared baking tray. Place in the fridge for 30 minutes.

Bake in the preheated oven for about 55 minutes, turning the tray round after 30 minutes and trying not to get much colour on the shortbread.

Once out of the oven, sprinkle with caster sugar, cool on the tray for a few minutes, then transfer to a cooling rack.

Get that kettle on!

MAKES ABOUT
32 BISCUITS

375g plain flour

250g cold butter, diced

65g caster sugar, plus extra for sprinkling

30g demerara sugar

30g soft light brown sugar

4g fine sea salt

YOU WILL NEED
a 6cm round pastry cutter

GELLATLY'S BANNOCK

Going back to before we baked in the oven, straight on the fire! Justin's father, William Gellatly, used to bake this over an open fire when they went camping, and Justin still bakes it today when he's on an overnight fishing trip. Serve with fried eggs as part of your campfire breakfast.

SERVES 4–8

a good piece of thick-cut fatty smoked bacon, about 200g

150g whole wheat flour

165g coarse or medium oatmeal

6g fine sea salt

155g water

Cut the bacon into small chunks, then place them in a cast-iron heavy-based frying pan about 24cm wide and slowly render down. Once the fat has been released, turn up the heat and fry the bacon until crispy and golden brown. Leave to cool in the pan.

Once the bacon is cool, add all the other ingredients to the pan and mix together until a dough is formed. Flatten the dough in the pan. Put the pan back on a medium heat with the lid on and cook for 10 minutes on each side. This is a very heavy bread that will set you up for the day.

You can also bake the bannock over an open fire, using a stick or a long skewer. Squeeze 130g of the dough round the top 12cm of the stick or skewer, like a kebab, and bake over the fire for about 30 minutes, turning every 5 minutes. Try not to let it get too dark – though it still tastes good with plenty of singe!

Dip it into your baked beans for a bean glaze 'boom'!

SPICED WELSH CAKES

These are traditionally baked on a bakestone or a flat griddle, but a heavy-based frying pan works just as well. It's best to eat them straight from the pan, while still hot.

Put the flour, salt and butter into a large bowl and rub together, using your fingertips, until the mixture looks like breadcrumbs. Add the mixed spice, allspice, sultanas and sugars and mix together well, then add the honey, followed by the beaten egg.

Now mix until all is combined, then bring together to form a dough (it will be a little sticky). Wrap it in cling film and pop it into the fridge to rest for 1 hour.

On a lightly floured work surface, roll out the dough to 1cm thick. Using a 6cm round pastry cutter, cut out 12 rounds, re-rolling your dough when necessary, and then put them on a lightly floured baking tray.

Heat a large (26cm) heavy-based non-stick frying pan on a medium heat and put half the Welsh cakes into the pan, making sure you don't overcrowd them. Don't be tempted to add any oil or butter – all it needs is that dry heat. Turn the heat down to low and cook the cakes for about 3–4 minutes on each side, until dark golden brown (but take care not to singe them too much). Then bake the second batch the same way.

Serve straight from pan to plate.

MAKES 12

225g self-raising flour, plus extra for dusting

a pinch of fine sea salt

125g unsalted butter, diced

½ teaspoon ground mixed spice

½ teaspoon ground allspice

125g sultanas

15g demerara sugar

80g caster sugar

20g fragrant pure honey

1 egg, beaten

YOU WILL NEED
a 6cm round pastry cutter

FLATBREADS

Flatbreads are made all over the world. They can be yeasted or non-yeasted, crispy or soft, thick or thin, puffed up or flat, and all shapes and sizes under the sun.

Leavened or not, these are among the most ancient kind of breads, and don't need an oven or even any utensils to be baked. This style of bread has been baked on open fires, ashes and hot stones since the beginning of time, when we first started to pound corn and to mill wheat.

These breads are very simple to make, often containing just three ingredients. Yoghurt is also a popular addition. You can use many different kinds of flour, from chickpea to cornmeal, and you can add any number of different types of herbs and spices.

From Middle Eastern flatbreads, to Armenian, Greek, Indian and many more, what the breads in this chapter all have in common is that they are generally used in place of a knife and fork – to scoop your food on to, to roll as a wrap, or to mop things up with.

SANGAK

Traditionally, these wholesome Iranian flatbreads were baked in the oven on a bed of small river stones. In Persian, the word 'sangak' literally translates to 'little stone', which is how this bread got its name.

DAY 1: Mix the starter and water together in a large bowl, then add the flour and salt. With your hand shaped like a fork, mix until evenly combined. Scrape the dough out of the bowl on to a work surface, then 'stretch and tear', using the technique described on page 18, for 1 minute. Drizzle some oil into the bowl, then pop the dough back in. Cover with a tea towel, cling film or a shower cap and leave to rest for 10 minutes.

Give the dough a fold, using the technique for folding in half described on page 21, then cover again as before, place in the fridge and leave for 8–24 hours.

DAY 2: Preheat the oven to 250°C/fan 230°C/gas 10, or as hot as it will go, and put a baking tray in to heat up.

Heavily flour your work surface. Take the dough out of the bowl and divide it into 4 equal pieces weighing about 110g each if using white flour and 2 pieces of 220g if using wholemeal. Pull each piece out to form a rectangle about 10cm x 20cm, then gently massage with your fingertips on the top of the dough to give it a dimpled effect (this will give your dough the appearance of being baked on stones). Note that the dough will be very sticky and might rip a little, but that's fine. Sprinkle with the seeds, if you like.

Take your hot baking tray out of the oven and lay one or two of your sangaks on it. Put back into the oven and bake for 3 minutes on each side for the white ones and 4 minutes each side for the wholemeal.

Serve warm, with grilled meats, wedges of lemon and bowls of salad.

MAKES 2 WHOLEMEAL OR 4 WHITE FLATBREADS

75g rye starter (see page 33)

150g cold water

200g strong white (or wholemeal) bread flour, plus extra for dusting

4g fine sea salt

a splash of olive oil, for the bowl

optional: sunflower and nigella seeds, for sprinkling

FLATBREADS / 244

GREEK PITTA

One of the most popular street foods in Greece. Justin and Louise fell in love with these when travelling round the Greek islands. The best one we had was on Naxos, from a little family-run taverna cum bakery. But with this recipe, we can all make our own delicious gyros at home. Don't forget to pack them to bursting with your chosen filling.

MAKES 7

300g water

5g fresh yeast

400g strong white bread flour, plus extra for dusting

7g fine sea salt

20g olive oil, plus extra for the bowl and frying

Put the water and yeast into a large bowl and stir to dissolve the yeast, then sift in the flour and the salt, and pour in the oil.

With one hand shaped like a fork, gently bring together until just combined. It should take only a couple of minutes. Scrape the dough off your hand into the bowl, then take the dough out of the bowl and place on a floured work surface, making sure you scrape all the dough out with a scraper to leave a clean bowl. Keep the bowl to one side, as you will need it later.

Now, with your dough on the work surface and you 'poised like a puma' (see page 18), with the heel of your hand push the dough into the work surface and 'stretch and tear', using the technique described on page 18, for about 6 minutes.

Lightly oil the bowl you used earlier and pop the dough back in, then give it a fold, using the technique described on page 21. After folding, leave it to rest for 15 minutes, then give the dough three more folds, resting for 15 minutes each time. Between folds you will need to cover the bowl with cling film, a tea towel or a shower cap. Leave in the bowl for another 15 minutes after the last fold.

Divide the dough into 7 pieces, each weighing 100g, and shape them into balls (the dough will be a bit sticky). Cover and leave for 10 minutes.

Heavily flour your work surface. Roll each ball into a 20cm round, then prick all over with a fork.

Heat a frying pan (it needs to be larger than 20cm), then add a little olive oil and carefully add one pitta. Fry on each side for 3 minutes, and repeat until all are cooked, covering them with a tea towel as you go.

Fill your gyros with roast chicken, salad, chips and mayonnaise, sprinkle with paprika, and then transport yourself to the streets of Greece.

ARABIAN PITTA

These classic Arabian flatbreads are a joy to make at home and are so much nicer than their packet counterparts.

Put the flour and salt into a bowl and mix together enough for them to get to know each other. Make a well in the centre.

Put the yeast (or rye starter) and water into another bowl and mix until dissolved.

Pour the yeasted water and the olive oil into the well in the flour, then gently bring the dough together. Once it starts coming together, take it out of the bowl and place it on your work surface. Don't add any flour.

Now, with the dough on your work surface and you 'poised like a puma' (see page 18), with the heel of your hand push the dough into the work surface and 'stretch and tear', using the technique described on page 18, for about 8 minutes, until it's nice and elasticated. Oil the bowl, then put the dough back in, cover and leave at room temperature for 1 hour (2 hours for the sourdough version).

Preheat the oven to 250°C/fan 230°C/gas 10, or as hot as it will go. Put a baking stone or upturned baking tray in to heat up.

Take your dough out of the bowl and divide it into 5 pieces about 80g each. Gently shape each piece into a round and leave to rest for 10 minutes.

One by one, dust your dough pieces with flour and place them on a floured work surface. Using a rolling pin, roll each one out into an oblong shape about 20cm x 12cm, dusting with flour as required along the way.

Slide your bread directly on to the hot stone or baking tray in the oven. You should get them all on to one tray, but use two if you need to. Bake for 5 minutes – your pitta should puff up during the process.

Take out of the oven and immediately cover with a cloth until cooled. Then split open, fill with roast meat, thinly sliced, and salad, and enjoy.

Pitta bread will keep for 3 or 4 days and freezes very well. To serve, defrost and pop it into the toaster for 3 minutes.

MAKES 5

250g strong white (or wholemeal) bread flour, plus extra for dusting

5g fine sea salt

6g fresh yeast or 12g rye starter (see page 33)

140g water

10g olive oil, plus extra for the bowl

YOU WILL NEED

a baking stone or an upturned baking tray

LAVASH

These paper-thin flatbreads are wonderfully versatile and great for entertaining. They're delicious filled, but are equally enticing made into wraps or served with dips.

Put the flour and salt into a bowl and mix together enough for them to get to know each other. Make a well in the centre of the flour.

Put the yeast and water into another bowl and stir until dissolved.

Pour the liquid into the well in the flour, add the yoghurt, then, with one hand shaped like a fork, gently bring together until just combined. It should take only a couple of minutes. Scrape the dough off your hand into the bowl, then take the dough out of the bowl and place on a work surface, making sure you scrape all the dough out with a scraper to leave a clean bowl. Keep the bowl to one side, as you will need it later.

Now, with your dough on the unfloured work surface and you 'poised like a puma' (see page 18), with the heel of your hand push the dough into the work surface and 'stretch and tear', using the technique described on page 18, for about 8 minutes, making sure you scrape your dough to the centre throughout the 'stretching and tearing' so that the dough develops evenly. It still will be very sticky. If you are using the nigella seeds, add them in the last minute of the 'stretch and tear'.

Drizzle the bowl you used earlier with the olive oil and put your dough back in. Cover and leave at room temperature for 30 minutes. Then take your dough out of the bowl and divide it into 8 equal pieces, about 50g each. Shape each piece into a round and place on a heavily floured work surface.

Heavily flour the top of the dough, then, using a rolling pin, roll each piece out as thin as you can, to about 25cm in diameter, dusting with flour as required along the way.

There is more than one way to cook these flatbreads:

MAKES 8

225g strong white bread flour, plus extra for dusting

8g fine sea salt

5g fresh yeast

100g water

70g natural yoghurt

optional: 1 teaspoon nigella or black mustard seeds

12g olive oil

YOU WILL NEED

a baking stone or an upturned baking tray (for the oven method)

OVEN METHOD

Place a baking stone or upturned baking tray in the oven and preheat the oven to 250°C/fan 230°C/gas 10, or as hot as it will go. One at a time, slide your bread directly on the hot stone or tray and bake for 90 seconds.

HOB METHOD

Place a heavy-based pan on a high heat and leave it until it's smoking. One at a time, put your bread into the pan and cook for 30 seconds, then turn it over and cook for an additional 30 seconds.

Once baked (this applies to both methods), pile them up and cover with a damp cloth. Once cooled, serve.

These flatbreads can be covered with a cloth and stored in the fridge for a couple of days.

CHAPATTIS

I (Louise) knock up the most amazing vegetable curries for the bakers and these chapattis go alongside – they never disappoint.

Pretty much no meal in India is complete without some form of flatbread, and the chapatti is the most popular. It's used for everything, from eating food from your plate instead of a knife and fork to mopping up the juices at the end of the meal.

Place the flour, yoghurt, oil and salt in a large bowl and mix together, then pour in the water. Using your hand like a fork, bring together until it forms a loose dough. Take out of the bowl and place on an unfloured work surface.

Now, with your dough on the work surface and you 'poised like a puma' (see page 18), with the heel of your hand push the dough into the work surface and 'stretch and tear', using the technique described on page 18, for about 5 minutes. Bring the dough back together with your scraper once it is soft and pliable.

Divide the dough into 4 equal pieces, about 56g each, and shape them into balls. Lightly sprinkle your work surface with flour and roll the balls out to make circles 20cm in diameter.

Now, with them all rolled out, it's time to start cooking. Place your griddle or heavy-based frying pan over a high heat. Your pan should be hot before you start. One at a time, cook the chapattis for about 90 seconds on each side – they will start to puff up and you should see some dark golden blisters on each side before you turn them over. If not, leave the chapatti for a few more seconds on each side. Cover with a tea towel and serve still warm, with curry, or freeze to use at a later date.

MAKES 4

120g chapatti flour, plus extra for dusting

30g natural yoghurt

20g sunflower oil

2g fine sea salt

50g water

ROASTED RYE FLATBREAD

Roasting the rye flour gives these breads a really delicious nutty taste.

First roast the rye flour. Preheat your oven to 250°C/fan 230°C/gas 10, or as hot as it will go, then spread the flour evenly over a baking tray and pop it into the oven for 10 minutes, stirring every 2 minutes. Make sure you have an extraction fan on or the window open, as it makes a fair bit of smoke. Once the flour is roasted, leave it to cool.

Put the cooled roasted rye flour into a large bowl with the plain flour and salt, and mix together just enough for them to get to know each other. Put the water and yeast into another bowl and whisk until the yeast is dissolved, then pour into the flour.

With one hand shaped like a fork, bring all the ingredients together and knead in the bowl until all are mixed through evenly. Shape into a ball, then cover with a tea towel, cling film or a shower cap and leave for 1 hour.

Now divide the dough into 8 pieces weighing about 85g each. Shape them into balls, dust with flour and then leave to rest for 10 minutes.

Roll each ball out to make a circle about 18cm across. Heat a frying pan to a medium to high heat, then lightly oil the pan and cook each flatbread for 2 minutes on each side. Pile them up and cover them with a tea towel once cooked, to keep them warm as you go.

MAKES 8

100g roasted rye flour (see method)

300g plain flour, plus extra for dusting

4g fine sea salt

300g water

6g fresh yeast

oil, for greasing

FLOUR TORTILLAS

Tortillas are the perfect accompaniment to any Mexican feast. Using this recipe you can now make your own, and of course they will taste better than bought ones.

MAKES 12

500g plain white flour, plus extra for dusting

6g fine sea salt

2 teaspoons baking powder

25g cold unsalted butter, cut into small pieces

400g water

Sift the flour, salt and baking powder into a large bowl and mix together just enough for them to get to know each other. Add the butter and rub it into the flour using your fingertips. It should be incorporated into the flour in a couple of minutes, and the mixture should resemble fine breadcrumbs.

Add the water and then, using your hand like a fork, bring everything together until it forms a loose dough. Take out of the bowl and place on a work surface.

Now, with your dough on the work surface and you 'poised like a puma' (see page 18), with the heel of your hand push the dough into the work surface for about 5 minutes, using the 'stretch and tear' technique described on page 18, until smooth and elastic. Then pop it back into the bowl, cover with a tea towel, cling film or a shower cap, and leave to rest for 30 minutes.

Uncover the bowl, scrape the dough out on to a lightly floured work surface, and divide it into 12 equal pieces, about 75g each. If you find the dough too sticky, just rub your hands with a little flour. Cover the pieces of dough with a damp cloth.

Taking one ball of dough at a time, dip it into a bowl of plain white flour, then, using the palm of your hand, flatten it. Start to roll the flattened dough into a circle about 20cm in diameter. Watch that it doesn't start sticking. If it does, just dust a little bit of flour on the work surface. Carry on until all the tortillas are rolled out, sprinkling flour between them as you stack them up, to stop them sticking together.

Now, with all your tortillas rolled out, it's time to start cooking. Place your griddle or heavy-based frying pan over a medium heat. Your pan should be hot before you start. One at a time, cook the tortillas for about 30 seconds on each side. You should see some dark golden blisters when you turn them over – if not, leave for a few more seconds on each side.

Pile them on top of each other, covering them with foil or a clean towel to keep them warm, and serve with a Mexican feast.

CORN TORTILLAS

If you have corn you have life! If you have corn you have tortillas.

Some recipes are trial and error; some involve a bit of luck and others are about being in the right place at the right time. On a recent trip to Madrid we stumbled upon a Mexican restaurant that made the real thing. We had previously made a few attempts at making corn tortillas that were hit and miss, but since our chat with the Mexicans we have seen the tortilla light.

The tortilla press, though not essential, is a very useful piece of kit – it makes a 2-minute job into a 20-second one that is consistent every time. You will need two A4 size sheets of silicon paper, or non-stick baking paper. The griddle for cooking is dry – no oil is used at all.

Quite simply, mix the water and cornmeal together in a bowl. All you need to do is bring them together into a paste using a wooden spoon. The tortilla mix itself is very slightly sticky, with the texture of plasticine. Leave the dough to rest for 30 minutes.

Scrape the dough out of the bowl on to a floured work surface. Divide it into walnut-size pieces (about 30g), making sure you keep them covered while you work. Place each ball of dough between two sheets of silicon/baking paper and flatten them with the tortilla press to about 10–12cm across. If you don't have a press, use a rolling pin. As they are ready, stack them on top of each other, sprinkling flour between them.

Now transfer your flattened tortillas to a hot dry pan. Cook each side for about 35–40 seconds, turning them with a spatula.

Once cooked, they should be piled up on top of one another and covered with a tea towel, but do serve them while they are still warm. We ate ours just with sea salt, as a starter, which was lovely.

MAKES 15

280g hot water

200g finely ground cornmeal (masa harina)

plain flour, for dusting

YOU WILL NEED

2 sheets of A4 size silicon or non-stick baking paper

optional: a tortilla press

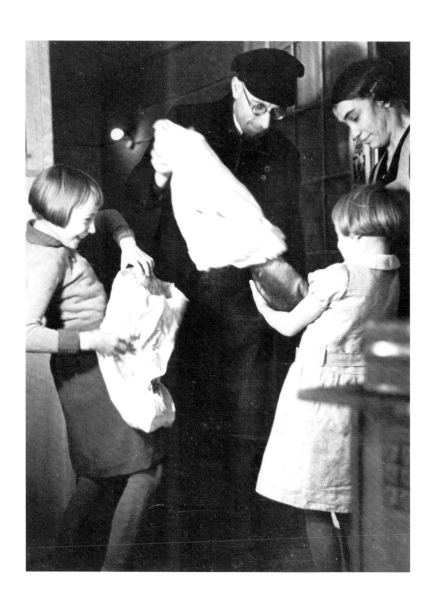

GLUTEN-FREE BAKING

We have aimed to make this chapter as simple as possible, using accessible ingredients and trying not to over-compensate with other flavours, leaving the bread to speak for itself. This chapter is not just for people who can't have gluten, as all the recipes are delicious in their own way.

As bakers, we normally just use three ingredients to make bread: flour, water and salt. But with gluten-free baking it's difficult to get that rise and open texture without using some form of natural stabilizer like eggs.

With all these recipes, don't be afraid to use them as starting blocks to change and experiment with. Try different flours and flavours, according to your own personal taste.

We do use specific brands in some of the recipes in this chapter, such as Doves Farm and Rude Health. This is because we feel, where stated, that the recipes work best with these specific products – they are all readily available in most shops with trolleys!

A CHEEKY BONNY GF SOURDOUGH

Surprisingly, buckwheat is part of the rhubarb family. We use buckwheat flour to make the starter for this gluten-free sourdough. It has an amazing tang to it and makes quite a special loaf, which we really love.

FOR THE STARTER: Mix 25g of buckwheat flour with 25g of cold water and leave at room temperature for 24 hours. Feed the starter by mixing in another 25g of buckwheat flour and 25g of water every day for 4 more days. On day 6 your starter will be ready to use.

8 hours before you want to make your bread, mix 50g of buckwheat flour and 50g of water into your starter (you need to do this every time you want to make your bread). You can store the starter for up to 2 weeks in the fridge.

On day 1, place all the pre-ferment ingredients in a bowl and mix together until fully combined. Leave at room temperature for 8 hours, or in the fridge for up to 24 hours.

Next day (day 2), pour the water into a large bowl, add your pre-ferment and mix together until the pre-ferment has broken down.

Add all the flours and the salt and mix together for a couple of minutes, then cover and leave for 10 minutes.

Uncover, remix, then carefully scrape the dough into an 18cm x 8cm x 6cm loaf tin lined with baking paper, trying to get the top nice and even. Sprinkle with chestnut flour, cover, and leave to rise for about 2½ hours. You want the dough to pretty much reach the top of the tin.

Preheat the oven to 230°C/fan 210°C/gas 8.

Once your dough has proved, place in the oven and bake for 30 minutes, then remove the loaf from the tin and put back into the oven, directly on the oven shelf, for a further 10 minutes.

Place on a rack to cool, then enjoy.

MAKES I SMALL LOAF

DAY I: THE PRE-FERMENT

100g gluten-free bread flour (we use Doves Farm)

80g starter (see method)

140g cold water

DAY 2

125g cold water

95g gluten-free bread flour

25g chestnut flour, plus extra for sprinkling

20g coconut flour

25g buckwheat flour

7g salt

THE COCONUT PIZZA BASE

These great pizzas take no time at all to make and bake. Now no one needs to miss out on delicious pizza. The coconut flour isn't overly sweet, and it gives a wonderful crust to the pizza base.

MAKES 2 SMALL PIZZAS

polenta or semolina, for dusting

80g gluten-free bread flour (we use Doves Farm), plus extra for dusting

20g coconut flour

4g fine sea salt

50g natural yoghurt

28g water

Mrs G's tomato sauce (see page 55)

your desired toppings, such as pesto and peppers

YOU WILL NEED

a baking stone or an upturned baking tray

a baker's peel or a wooden board or flat baking sheet

Preheat the oven to 240°C/fan 220°C/gas 9 and put a baking stone or an upturned baking tray in to heat up. Sprinkle a baker's peel, wooden board or flat baking sheet with polenta or semolina.

Combine the flours, salt, yoghurt and water in a large bowl and work the dough for 2 minutes until you have a firm, moist but pliable dough. Leave to rest for 5 minutes, then work the dough for a further 2 minutes and leave to rest for 20 minutes.

After resting, place the dough on a lightly floured surface and divide it in half. Pat each half down to about 5mm or a little thinner to form your pizzas. Once shaped, place them carefully on the prepared peel, wooden board or flat baking sheet.

You can put your toppings on now, then slide the pizzas off the peel on to the baking stone or upturned baking tray in the oven and bake for about 6–8 minutes. But for a crispier base, slide in the pizza bases before adding any toppings, and bake for 5 minutes. Take them out and pop your toppings on, then slide them back in and bake for a further 3–4 minutes.

Eat while still hot!

FLATBREADS

This easy-peasy recipe is really simple – it's a great one to pull out of the bag for a light snack or a dinner party.

Combine the flour, yoghurt and salt in a large bowl and work for a few minutes until you have a firm, moist but pliable dough. Leave to rest for 5 minutes, then work the dough for a further couple of minutes and leave to rest for 20 more minutes.

Preheat the oven to 240°C/fan 220°C/gas 9, and line a baking tray with baking paper.

After the dough has rested, divide it into 4 equal pieces about 180g each. Using your hand to press down the dough, shape each piece into a rough circle about 20cm in diameter. Very carefully place your circles on the lined baking tray, lightly brush with water and sprinkle with the seeds. Bake for 8 minutes, turning them over halfway through.

Once baked, leave to cool on a rack, and serve with dips galore!

MAKES 4 GLORIOUS, FLAVOURSOME BREADS

400g gluten-free bread flour (we use Doves Farm)

310g natural yoghurt

14g fine sea salt

sesame and poppy seeds, for the top

WHITE TIN BREAD

Well, this is pretty much as close as we could get to a handsome soft crusty white tin, and, to be honest, we would happily have this for our breakfast with a couple of rashers of bacon.

420g gluten-free bread flour (we use Doves Farm)

10g baking powder

8g fine sea salt

315g water

10g fresh yeast

5g pure honey

2 eggs

40g olive oil

Sift the flour, baking powder and salt into a large bowl. Put the water and yeast into another bowl and stir to dissolve the yeast, then mix in the honey.

Crack the eggs into a third bowl and whisk them with the olive oil. Stir the egg mix into the flour mix, then slowly add the water mix, whisking until everything is combined evenly into a dough. Cover the bowl and leave to prove for 30 minutes. While it is proving, line a bread tin 20cm x 10cm x 6cm.

When the 30 minutes is up, scrape the dough into the tin and smooth the top. Cover with cling film or a shower cap and leave to prove for about 40 minutes, until the dough is nearly up to the top of the tin.

Preheat the oven to 220°C/fan 200°C/gas 7.

Once your dough has risen, uncover it and place in the oven for 40 minutes. Then take it out of the tin, put the loaf back into the oven, directly on the oven shelf, and bake for a further 5 minutes.

Cool on a rack, and use to make toast or delicious sandwiches.

CHESTNUT BREADSTICKS

These classic Italian breadsticks work perfectly made with a mix of gluten-free flours.

On day 1, make the poolish. Place the water in a small container, then add the yeast and mix until it has dissolved. Add the flour and combine fully. Cover and place in the fridge for 12–18 hours.

Next day (day 2), put the water and yeast into a bowl and mix together until the yeast has dissolved.

Place the flours and salt in a large bowl and mix together, just enough for them to get to know each other.

Uncover your poolish from the day before – it will be nice and bubbly and will have a lovely aroma to it. Add the yeast mix and the poolish to the flour, then with one hand mix together to form a stiff dough. Add the chopped rosemary and mix it into your dough.

Preheat your oven to 150°C/fan 130°C/gas 2.

Once the dough has come together and the rosemary is mixed through evenly, take small pieces of the dough (about 12g) and roll out each one thinly to about 18cm long, being careful not to tear them.

Place the sticks on a tray dusted with fine polenta, then brush them with olive oil and sprinkle with crunchy coarse sea salt.

Bake for 20 minutes, then turn the tray round and bake for a further 8 minutes.

Leave to cool, and either serve with dips or enjoy them on their own as a delicious snack.

MAKES ABOUT 14 BREADSTICKS

DAY 1: THE POOLISH (SEE PAGE 15)

40g cold water

2g fresh yeast

25g chestnut flour

DAY 2

60g cold water

1g fresh yeast

100g gluten-free bread flour (we use Doves Farm)

25g chestnut flour

2g salt

1 teaspoon chopped rosemary

fine polenta, for dusting

olive oil, for brushing

crunchy coarse sea salt, for sprinkling

DOUGHNUTS (YES, DOUGHNUTS!)

We make these doughnuts with Rude Health buckwheat flour – the depth of flavour is quite brilliant, and people often don't realize that the doughnuts are gluten-free. They are really moist and delicious, with or without the glaze.

MAKES 12 DOUGHNUTS

70g unsalted butter

40g pure honey

160g buckwheat flour
(we use Rude Health)

1 teaspoon fine sea salt

1 teaspoon baking powder

65g soft light brown
sugar

125g ground almonds

2 eggs, beaten

195g natural yoghurt

50g milk

2 teaspoons vanilla
extract

THE CLASSIC GLAZE

1 vanilla pod

50g butter

180g icing sugar

4 tablespoons milk

YOU WILL NEED

a non-stick doughnut
mould

On a low heat, melt the butter and honey together in a pan, then leave to cool for a few minutes.

Sift the flour, salt and baking powder into a large bowl, then add the sugar and ground almonds and whisk together for 20 seconds. Now add the beaten eggs, yoghurt, milk, vanilla and the melted butter mix and whisk to combine. Leave to rest for 10 minutes.

Preheat your oven to 180°C/fan 160°C/gas 4.

Pour 60g of mixture into each doughnut mould and bake in the preheated oven for 8 minutes, or until firm to the touch.

Place the tray on a cooling rack and leave for 2 minutes before turning out.

Eat warm, straight away, or leave the doughnuts to cool a little more before glazing.

To make the glaze, slit the vanilla pod open lengthways and scrape out the seeds. Put the seeds and pod into a heavy-based saucepan with the butter, and slowly melt over a low heat to infuse the vanilla.

Sift the icing sugar into a bowl, then take out the vanilla pod and whisk in the vanilla butter and the milk to make the glaze.

COOKIES

These cookies are bloody delicious and very moreish – one is never enough. We love the way the currants are all chewy throughout the cookie. You can substitute an equal amount of black treacle for the golden syrup, to give you less sweetness and a depth of flavour, which we love, but it's not to everyone's taste.

Put the black treacle and golden syrup into a saucepan and add the butter. Melt together on a medium heat, then leave to cool for 10 minutes.

Put the flours, bicarbonate of soda, oats, salt, mixed peel, sugars and currants into a large mixing bowl. Add the treacle mix, making sure you scrape it all out. Mix everything together to form a paste-like dough, making sure all is combined well.

Preheat your oven to 160°C/fan 140°C/gas 3 and line a few baking trays with baking paper.

Divide the mixture into 40g balls and place on the prepared baking trays. Gently press each one down to form a flat cookie, making sure you leave plenty of space between them, as they will spread.

Bake in the oven for about 20 minutes, turning the trays round after 10 minutes.

Cool on the tray for a while, then carefully place them on a rack to cool completely.

MAKES 18 MOREISH COOKIES

45g black treacle

55g golden syrup

120g unsalted butter

100g gluten-free bread flour (we use Doves Farm)

50g coconut flour

1 teaspoon bicarbonate of soda

100g jumbo oats

1 teaspoon fine sea salt

30g mixed peel

100g caster sugar

50g demerara sugar

110g currants

GLUTEN-FREE 'FRUIT AND NUT' BROWNIES

These brownies are dark, rich and moist and are a real treat.

Preheat your oven to 180°C/fan 160°C/gas 4. Lightly grease a 38cm x 25cm x 2cm baking tray and line it with baking paper.

Put the butter and 400g of the chocolate into a heatproof bowl over a pan of lightly simmering water and leave to melt slowly. Break the remaining 100g of chocolate into chunks.

While the chocolate is melting, mix the eggs and sugar in a large bowl, using a whisk to beat them together for about 2–3 minutes. Once the chocolate has melted, pour it over the egg mix and whisk together briefly, then fold in the sifted baking powder and add the 100g of chocolate chunks, the hazelnuts, raisins and salt.

Pour the mixture into the prepared baking tray and bake for 25 minutes.

Take out of the oven and place on a cooling rack for 1 hour – it might look a little under-baked but as it cools down it will firm up.

Serve warm with ice cream, or (our favourite) pop it into the fridge overnight and have chilled as a chocolate bar.

MAKES ABOUT 20

300g unsalted butter, plus extra for greasing

500g chocolate, broken up

6 eggs

500g caster sugar

1 teaspoon baking powder

125g ground hazelnuts

180g hazelnuts

180g raisins

4g fine sea salt

LEMON POLENTA CAKE

This is a very moist cake which is actually better when you bake it the day before you need it. You can change the flavour from lemon to orange if you prefer.

SERVES 8–12

300g ground almonds

100g fine polenta/cornmeal

50g coarse polenta

1 teaspoon baking powder

300g butter, plus extra for greasing

zest and juice of 2 lemons

300g caster sugar

4 eggs

Preheat the oven to 180°C/fan 160°C/gas 4. Grease and line a 20cm loose-bottomed round cake tin.

Mix the almonds, both kinds of polenta and the baking powder together in a bowl and set aside.

Put the butter, lemon zest and sugar into a larger bowl and cream together until they start to turn pale and fluffy. Add the eggs slowly, one at a time, and gently mix in. If your mixture starts to curdle, add a little of your polenta mix and stir in to rescue it.

Once you have added all the eggs, add all the polenta mixture. Mix until fully combined, then add the juice of the lemons and mix for another minute. Pour into the prepared cake tin and smooth the top.

Bake for 55 minutes, turning the tin once, halfway through.

Take out of the oven and cool for 5 minutes, then remove from the tin and place on a rack to cool. Enjoy with a good dollop of whipped cream.

COCONUT AND HAZELNUT SLICE

The perfect cake for afternoon tea.

Preheat your oven to 180°C/fan 160°C/gas 4. Line a 30cm x 20cm x 4cm baking tin with baking paper.

Put the eggs, orange zest and sugar into a large mixing bowl and whisk together until the volume has tripled and the mixture looks thick, light and fluffy.

In another bowl, sift the baking powder into the coconut flour and ground hazelnuts and whisk together.

Add the ground hazelnut mix to the egg mix, and gently fold together until all is incorporated.

Pour the mixture into your prepared baking tin and sprinkle heavily with coconut flakes. Bake for about 18–20 minutes, until golden brown and firm to the touch.

SERVES ABOUT 8, WITH A COUPLE OF PIECES EACH

6 eggs

zest of 1 orange

200g demerara sugar

10g baking powder

150g coconut flour

150g ground hazelnuts

coconut flakes, to decorate

PUFF PASTRY

Gosh, the beauty of puff pastry, the crispy, flaky buttered layers that make everything from tarts to palmiers. It's so versatile, and it's great to have in the freezer, which means it is always ready to pull out of the bag.

Don't be put off by the length of time it takes to make – once you have mastered it and made it a few times you will wonder why you've never made it before. It's a great skill to have, and if you make it yourself it always tastes better than the shop-bought versions.

Don't be scared of the amount of butter in our recipe – it's there for a reason. As the butter melts in the hot oven it produces steam, bringing the puff to life, making it rise into the air. The butter is crucial for the rise, the layers and also for the taste – never go down the margarine route, it's all about the butter!

PUFF PASTRY

Place the flour, salt and diced cold butter in the bowl of an electric mixer fitted with the beater attachment, and mix on slow speed until the mixture looks like fine breadcrumbs.

Change the attachment to the dough hook. Add the cold water and vinegar to the flour mix, and mix on a medium speed for about 2 minutes. The dough should feel nice and pliable.

Alternatively, place the flour, salt and diced cold butter in a bowl and rub the butter into the flour, using your fingertips, until the mixture looks like fine breadcrumbs. Add the cold water and vinegar and mix together until a dough is formed.

Take the dough out of the bowl, wrap it in cling film and put it into the fridge to rest for at least 2 hours, ideally overnight.

When your dough has chilled enough, take the second quantity of butter out of the fridge to soften. When it's been out for 30–40 minutes or so, take out the dough. The dough and butter need to be the same softness (this is very important).

Roll out the dough on a lightly floured surface into the shape of a cross measuring about 45cm, leaving the centre thicker than the flaps which make the arms of the cross. Dot the softened butter evenly over the centre of the dough and fold over the flaps or 'arms' to enclose it. Fold over the top and bottom flaps first, then cover with the side flaps to make sure no butter is showing. If the flaps are not long enough to cover the butter, just roll them out a little longer.

Start rolling lengthways until you have a strip about 70cm long and 25cm wide, brushing off any excess flour. Make sure all the sides are straight. With one of the shorter sides nearest you, fold it into thirds, first bottom to middle, then top to bottom. This finishes the first turn.

Turn the pastry so that the seam or join is always on its right and roll it out again before folding just as before. This is the second turn. Wrap the pastry in cling film and put it into the fridge for 3 hours.

Repeat another two turns as above, again resting for 3 hours. Finally, do a final two turns so that you have done six turns in total.

Rest the pastry again, then use for the recipes overleaf.

MAKES A MIGHTY 2.5KG, BUT IT FREEZES REALLY WELL

1kg strong white bread flour, plus extra for dusting

15g fine sea salt

250g cold unsalted butter, diced

450g cold water

25g white wine vinegar

750g softened unsalted butter

BREAD AHEAD SAUSAGE ROLLS

A firm English favourite, these are also very popular with everyone at Bread Ahead.

MAKES 6 OR
25 PARTY SIZE

500g puff pastry
(see page 278)

1 egg yolk, beaten, to seal

THE FILLING

400g plain sausagemeat

50g minced pork

3 tablespoons finely
chopped onions

5g garlic flakes

1 tablespoon onion powder

2 tablespoons ground
mace

4 tablespoons chopped
curly parsley

2 teaspoons chopped
thyme leaves

2 teaspoons English
mustard powder

1½ teaspoons fine sea salt

1 teaspoon ground
white pepper

1 teaspoon ground allspice

1 tablespoon garlic
granules

SPRINKLES

crunchy sea salt flakes,
black onion seeds, mustard
seeds, fennel seeds, diced
smoked pancetta

The day before you want to make your sausage rolls, place all the filling ingredients in a large bowl, and mix together using your hands, really massaging the meat with all the spices and other ingredients. Cover with cling film and leave in the fridge overnight – this will help all those delicious ingredients to get to know each other!

Next day, on a lightly floured work surface, roll out the puff pastry into a 45cm x 32cm rectangle and cut it in half lengthways. Lay the pieces next to each other lengthways.

Spread the filling in an even line along each rectangle, leaving a 3cm gap round the edge, shaping it into a sort of sausage shape along the puff pastry.

Brush all the edges of the puff pastry with egg yolk, then fold one side of the pastry over to join the other side and enclose the sausage mixture. Press the pastry down round the edges, then use the back of a fork dipped in flour to press down along the seam and seal the join. Pop back into the fridge for 2 hours to firm up the pastry.

Take out of the fridge and brush with more egg yolk, then cut into sausage rolls of your desired size. Place them on a lined baking tray, leaving a bit of space between them. If you feel like sprinkling, try something like crunchy sea salt flakes, black onion seeds, mustard seeds, fennel seeds or some cheeky diced smoked pancetta.

Preheat the oven to 200°C/fan 180°C/gas 6. Bake smaller sausage rolls for 20 minutes and larger ones for about 40 minutes, until crispy golden brown and hot throughout.

CHEESE, MUSTARD AND CAYENNE STRAWS/ DRIED SHRIMP AND SESAME STRAWS

These cheese straws are perfect for any soirée – make both varieties and serve in glasses for the full effect.

On a lightly floured work surface, roll out the puff pastry to a 90cm x 35cm rectangle.

To make the cheese, mustard and cayenne straws: with the longest edge nearest to you, spread the Dijon mustard evenly over the rolled-out pastry, right to the edges. Sprinkle the left-hand half of the pastry with the grated cheese and cayenne (depending on how spicy hot you want them). Fold the half without cheese over the other half and press down to seal, then place on a baking tray lined with baking paper and chill in the fridge until firm.

To make the dried shrimp and sesame straws: soak the dried shrimps in just-boiled water for 15 minutes, to rehydrate them. Strain and give them a squeeze to get rid of any excess water. Chop the shrimps (not too small, just run a knife through them once). With the longest edge nearest to you, brush the whole of the pastry with the beaten egg white. Sprinkle the left-hand half of the pastry with the grated cheese , along with the shrimps and a few hot chilli flakes, then fold the half without filling over the other half and press down to seal. Place on a baking tray lined with baking paper and chill in the fridge until firm.

Once firm, place the pastry on a board. Brush with eggwash and sprinkle with sesame seeds if making the dried shrimp and sesame straws. Slice the pastry into long straws, twist them gently, and lay them on a baking tray lined with baking paper (you can use the same one as before), leaving a little space between them.

Preheat the oven to 180°C/fan 160°C/gas 4. Bake the straws until golden brown, which should take 16–18 minutes for the cheese, mustard and cayenne version and 18–20 minutes for the dried shrimp and sesame one.

Remember to have some chilled bubbles in the fridge ready to go.

MAKES 24

plain flour, for dusting

500g puff pastry (see page 278)

1 egg, beaten, for the eggwash

THE CHEESE FILLING

2 tablespoons Dijon mustard

200g grated cheese

a good sprinkle of cayenne pepper

THE DRIED SHRIMP FILLING

2 teaspoons dried shrimps

1 egg white, beaten

150g grated cheese

100g dried chilli flakes

sesame seeds, for sprinkling

ECCLES CAKES

These are lovely, and are even more so served with a wedge of cheese.

MAKES 14

750g puff pastry
(see page 278)

plain flour, for dusting

1 egg, beaten, for
the eggwash

caster sugar, for
sprinkling

THE FILLING

125g softened
unsalted butter

90g soft dark
brown sugar

25g soft light
brown sugar

25g demerara sugar

250g currants

juice of 1 lemon

a pinch of salt

2g ground allspice

2g ground nutmeg

2g ground cinnamon

2g ground mixed spice

YOU WILL NEED

a 7½cm round
pastry cutter

In a large bowl, mix all the filling ingredients together until incorporated evenly, then chill in the fridge for a couple of hours.

Once chilled, roll the mixture into balls about 40g in weight and flatten them down so each resembles an ice hockey puck, then pop them into the fridge to firm up a little more.

Roll out the pastry on a lightly floured surface, to 1½cm thick.

Cut discs out of the pastry using a 7½cm round pastry cutter, then place a 'puck' of Eccles mix in the centre of each one. Pull up the sides of the pastry to cover the filling and seal together so that no filling is showing. Turn them over, place them on a baking tray lined with baking paper, leaving some space between them, and put back into the fridge for another hour.

Preheat your oven to 200°C/fan 180°C/gas 6.

Take your Eccles cakes out of the fridge and eggwash them generously all over. Slash the top three times with a sharp knife, then sprinkle them with caster sugar and bake for 35–40 minutes, until golden brown and oozing molten caramel deliciousness.

Leave to cool, and serve with a wedge of cheese, or simply with a mug of tea.

PALMIERS

Also known as pig's ears or elephant ears, these are crispy, buttery delights.

On a flour-dusted work surface, roll the pastry out to a 55cm x 30cm rectangle. Make sure the shortest length is facing you and the longest lengths are the sides. Whisk the egg white until the white has broken down and brush it all over the rolled-out pastry, then sprinkle heavily with about a third of the caster sugar.

Fold the bottom and top ends over so they meet in the middle, then once more brush with egg white and sprinkle with another third of the caster sugar. Repeat the folding a second time.

Fold the bottom end over the top end and press together (like a book), then wrap tightly in cling film and pop into the fridge to rest and firm up for at least 2 hours, and ideally overnight.

Take the dough out of the fridge, uncover and place on a board. Preheat your oven to 180°C/fan 160°C/gas 4.

Cut out the palmiers so that they are about 1cm in thickness and toss each one in caster sugar. Place them on a baking tray lined with baking paper, with some space between them.

Bake for 10 minutes, then take them out of the oven and turn them over. They should have started to caramelize underneath – if not, pop them back into the oven for another 2 minutes without turning them. Once you have turned over your palmiers, put them back into the oven for a further 4–5 minutes, until crispy and shining golden brown.

Once baked, leave to cool on the tray.

MAKES 30

plain flour, for dusting

500g puff pastry
(see page 278)

1 egg white

200g caster sugar,
plus extra for dusting

THE BREAD AHEAD PITHIVIER

The pithivier is traditionally served when celebrating the feast of the Epiphany on 6 January. A special charm is added to the filling, and whoever finds the charm is King or Queen for the day.

SERVES 4–6

12 prunes in Armagnac (place the pitted prunes in a jar and cover with Armagnac, then leave overnight or, even better, for a few months – we always have a jar or two on the go)

350g frangipane (see page 144)

650g puff pastry (see page 278)

plain flour, for dusting

1 egg yolk, beaten, for the eggwash

Chop your soaked prunes and mix them with the frangipane.

Put your pastry on a lightly floured work surface and cut it in half. Roll out the first piece of pastry to about 3–4mm thick, then, using a plate as a guide, cut out a circle about 26cm in diameter. Roll out the second piece and cut another circle, 30cm in diameter.

Place the smaller circle on a baking tray lined with baking paper. Spread the frangipane from the centre evenly over the base, leaving a 4cm margin round the edge. Brush the pastry edge with some of the eggwash.

Carefully lay the larger pastry circle over the top of the almond paste, pressing the edges of the two circles together firmly.

Place an upside-down 26cm plate over the centre of the pithivier, then press down gently and cut round the rim of the plate through the pastry. Take away the excess pastry.

Eggwash the whole pithivier, then, with a very sharp knife, make curved cuts 1mm deep in the pastry (be careful not to go all the way through), radiating from the centre of the pithivier right to the edge. Crimp the edges of the pithivier and pop it into the fridge for 1 hour to firm up.

Preheat your oven to 200°C/fan 180°C/gas 6.

Give your pithivier another eggwash, and bake for 25 minutes, until the pastry has a beautiful, shiny finish.

Once baked, place on a rack to cool. Serve with lashings of cold whipped cream, and any leftover Armagnac syrup from the jar, if you like.

CREAM HORNS

These 1950s classics come originally from Russia. You can also use the pastry horns as ice cream cones.

First grease your cream horn moulds by rubbing oil all over them.

On a lightly floured work surface, roll out the pastry into a 36cm x 46cm rectangle. Brush off any excess flour and, with the short side nearest to you, use a sharp knife to trim the edges nice and straight. Cut the pastry lengthwise into 10 strips 3cm wide.

Starting with the pointed end of a cream horn mould, start to wrap a strip of puff pastry round the mould in a spiral fashion, with each spiral overlapping slightly, then fold the top of the pastry inside the mould. Place wide side down on a baking tray lined with baking paper, then repeat until all the horns are covered in spiralling puff. Put them into the fridge to rest and firm up for about 1 hour.

Preheat your oven to 200°C/fan 180°C/gas 6.

Take the horns out of the fridge, brush them with eggwash, then roll them in about a third of the caster sugar and put them back on the lined baking tray.

Bake in the preheated oven for 12 minutes, until the pastry has risen, then take them out of the oven and turn the temperature down to 160°C/fan 140°C/gas 3. Carefully remove the moulds, leaving the puff pastry horns. Put them back into the oven for 10–12 minutes, just to crisp up the inside of your horns, then remove and place on a cooling rack.

Split the vanilla pod open lengthways and scrape out the seeds. Put the vanilla seeds into a bowl with the cream and the remaining sugar and whip to a gentle soft peak. Place in a piping bag.

Once cool, pipe the cream into your horns, sprinkle them with sugar-coated fennel seeds, and enjoy them freshly made.

MAKES 10

oil, for greasing

plain flour, for dusting

500g puff pastry
(see page 278)

1 egg, beaten, for
the eggwash

150g caster sugar

1 vanilla pod

500ml double cream

50g sugar-coated
fennel seeds

YOU WILL NEED

10 cylindrical 14cm
cream horn moulds

a piping bag

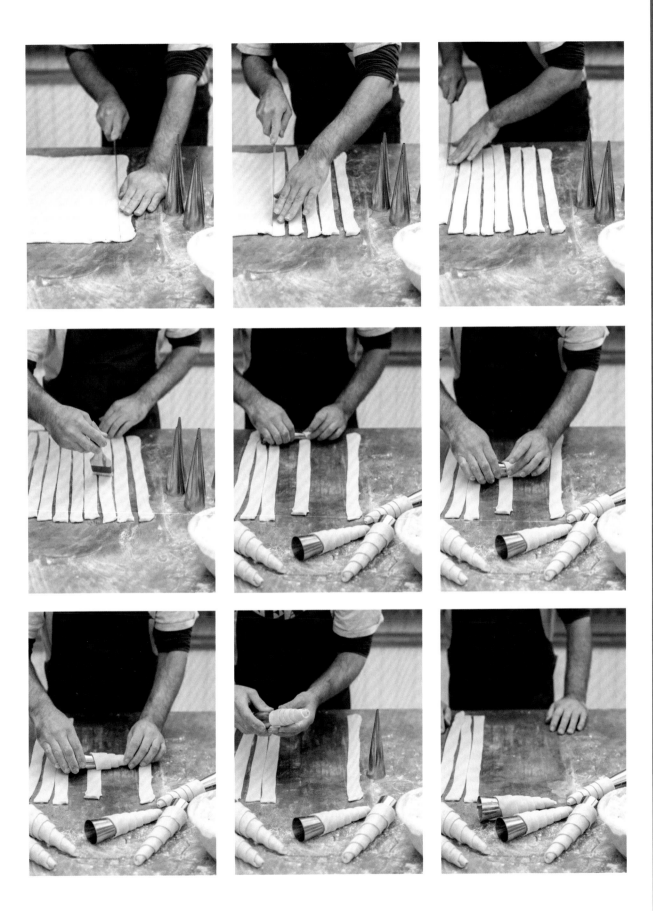

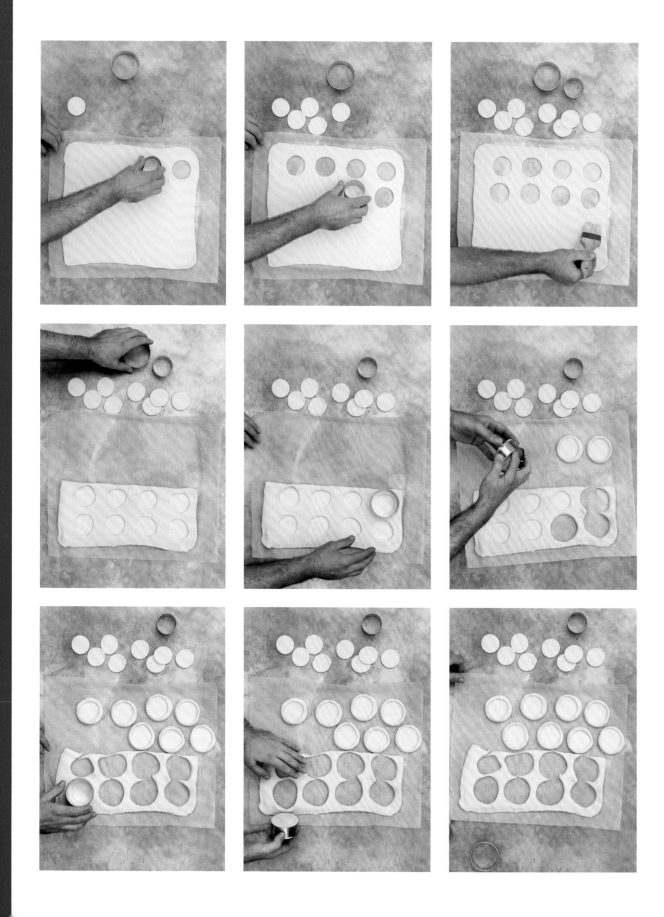

VOL-AU-VENTS

'Vol-au-vent' means 'flight on the wind', which describes the light buttery puff pastry here. There are 1,001 different fillings that you can use, but our favourite is Coronation chicken.

MAKES 8 – A FEW
MORE IF YOU RE-ROLL
THE PASTRY

500g puff pastry
(see page 278)

plain flour, for dusting

1 egg, beaten, for
the eggwash

YOU WILL NEED
5cm and 7cm round
pastry cutters

Roll out your pastry on a lightly floured work surface to a 32cm x 26cm rectangle. With the shorter side facing you, using a 5cm round pastry cutter, cut out 8 holes on just the left-hand side of the pastry, and place the cut-out discs to one side. Lightly brush the side of the pastry containing the holes with water and fold the uncut side over the cut side, then flip over so the side with the holes is on top.

Take a 7cm round pastry cutter, centre it over each of the cut holes, then cut through both layers. Place your cut-outs on a baking tray lined with baking paper, leaving some space between them. Prick the centre of each 7cm disc with a fork, then eggwash the top of the outside ring of pastry and place in the fridge for 1 hour. Place the smaller (5cm) discs on a separate lined baking tray, eggwash the tops, and put them into the fridge with the others for 1 hour.

Preheat the oven to 180°C/fan 160°C/gas 4. When ready to bake, eggwash the discs again for a richer colour and extra crispness, then place the two trays in the preheated oven, with the larger discs on the top shelf. Bake for 15 minutes, then take the tray with the smaller discs out. They should be golden brown, puffed up and flaky. Bring the top tray to the bottom of the oven and bake for a further 6 minutes – again they should be golden brown, puffed up and flaky.

Once baked, place the vol-au-vents on a rack to cool, then spoon in your desired filling – for example, fried wild mushrooms, prawn cocktail, smoked salmon and cream cheese, or spiced tomato aubergine. Top with the small pastry discs.

BOUCHÉES À LA REINE:
For a mini version, follow the recipe for vol-au-vents above, but use 2cm and 4cm cutters. Reduce the baking time to 10 minutes, plus a further 6 minutes.

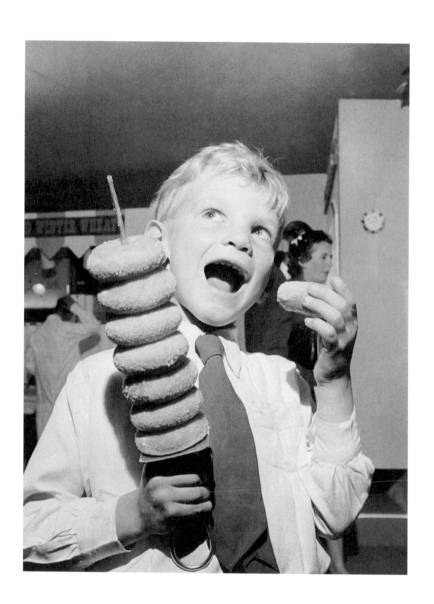

DOUGHNUTS
AKA 'PILLOWS OF JOY'

So many different people and countries claim to have invented the doughnut that it's hard to know for sure where they first came from. While we think of them as America's favourite snack, their origins are most likely Dutch. But with the US selling over 10 billion doughnuts each year, wherever they came from it's clear that these babies are here to stay.

Our own Bread Ahead doughnuts have become legendary in their own right, lovingly described as 'pillows of joy' and 'custard grenades'. We sell thousands on our Borough Market stall every weekend, and people travel from all over to try them.

We give these bad boys a long fermentation, to bleed out the lemon zest into the dough and really bring that flavour together. They are perfectly sweetened and enriched, then carpet-bombed with sugar to really get that lick-o'-lip factor. Then in goes the filling, piped to bursting and (our favourite) topped with that salted honeycomb!

We recommend using a deep-fat fryer (you can buy these for about £30), as it is a lot safer than a pan of hot oil. Deep-fat fryers have integral thermometers, so if you aren't using one you will need a good digital thermometer to check that the oil is at the right temperature. You will also need an electric mixer such as a Kenwood or a KitchenAid for the dough.

Eating a warm doughnut, freshly sugared and just out of the fryer, really is WOW! It's an experience normally reserved for the baker and for the students who come to Bread Ahead's Doughnut Masterclass. But now you can get to make your own 'pillows of joy' at home, and enjoy them fresh from the fryer.

THE DOUGHNUT DOUGH

It took us a long time to get this recipe perfect, but now you get to enjoy our hard work.

Place all the ingredients for the dough apart from the butter in the bowl of an electric mixer. Using the beater attachment, mix on medium speed for 6–8 minutes, or until the dough starts to come away from the sides and form a ball. Then turn off the mixer and let the dough rest for 1 minute. Start the mixer up again on a medium speed and slowly add the butter about 25g at a time. Once the butter is all incorporated, mix on high speed for a couple of minutes until the dough is glossy, smooth and elastic when pulled, then cover the bowl with cling film and leave to prove until it has doubled in size. Knock back the dough, re-cover and put into the fridge to chill overnight.

Next day, cut the dough into 50g pieces and roll them into smooth, tight buns (see page 25). Place them on a floured baking tray, leaving plenty of space between them so they don't stick together as they prove. Cover lightly with cling film and leave to prove for about 3–4 hours, or until they are approximately double in size. Get your deep-fat fryer ready, or get a heavy-based saucepan and fill it halfway up with sunflower oil (be careful, as hot oil is very dangerous). Heat the oil to 180°C.

Carefully remove the doughnuts from the tray by using a floured pastry scraper underneath them, and place in the oil. Do not overcrowd the fryer. Fry for 2 minutes on each side, until golden brown, then remove and place on kitchen paper. Toss the doughnuts in caster sugar while still warm from the fryer, making sure that you carpet-bomb them with sugar. Repeat until all the doughnuts are fried, but make sure the oil temperature is correct each time you fry – if it is too high they will colour too quickly and burn, but will be raw in the middle, and if it is too low the oil will be absorbed into the doughnut and it will become greasy.

To fill your doughnuts, make a hole in the side anywhere round the white line between the fried top and bottom (we like to call this the 'band of truth'). Fill a piping bag with your desired filling (see following pages) and pipe into the doughnuts until swollen. About 20–50g is the optimum quantity, depending on the type of filling (you need less cream than jam, because the cream is more aerated).

MAKES 20 DOUGHNUTS

sunflower oil, for deep frying

caster sugar, for tossing

THE DOUGH
500g strong white bread flour, plus extra for dusting

60g caster sugar

10g fine sea salt

15g fresh yeast

4 eggs

zest of 1 lemon

150g water

125g softened unsalted butter

YOU WILL NEED

a piping bag to fill your doughnuts (see fillings on following pages)

CLASSIC VANILLA CUSTARD

MAKES ENOUGH TO
FILL 20 DOUGHNUTS
GENEROUSLY

1 vanilla pod

1 litre full fat milk

12 egg yolks

175g caster sugar

75g plain white flour

250ml double cream

Slit the vanilla pod open lengthways and scrape out the seeds. Put the seeds and pod into a heavy-based saucepan with the milk and bring slowly to the boil, to infuse the vanilla.

Meanwhile, place the egg yolks and 125g of the sugar in a bowl and mix together for a few seconds, then sift in the flour and mix together.

Pour the boiling milk over the yolk mixture, whisking constantly to prevent curdling, then return the mixture to the saucepan and cook over a medium heat, whisking constantly for about 3 minutes, until nice and thick. Pass through a fine sieve, then place a sheet of cling film on the surface of the custard to prevent a skin forming (don't forget to keep your vanilla pod – wash and dry it to use again). Leave the custard to cool, then refrigerate. Whip the cream and remaining 50g of sugar together until thick and fold into the chilled custard.

RASPBERRY JAM

MAKES ENOUGH TO
FILL 20 DOUGHNUTS
GENEROUSLY

800g jam sugar

1kg raspberries

juice of 2 lemons

YOU WILL NEED

optional: a kitchen
thermometer

Preheat the oven to 120°C/fan 100°C/gas ½.

Put the sugar into a roasting tray and warm it in the oven for about 25 minutes. While the sugar is warming, put the raspberries and lemon juice into a preserving pan or an 8 litre saucepan and bring to a light simmer over a medium heat. Once this point has been reached, turn down the heat to low and gradually stir in the sugar. Once it has dissolved (which should happen quickly, as it is already warm), bring to the boil and simmer until setting point is reached – this can take anywhere from 20 to 30 minutes, depending on how juicy your raspberries are.

To test whether or not your jam has reached setting point, take a teaspoon of jam and place it on a cold plate. Allow to cool, then run your finger through it and if it doesn't run back on to itself, the setting point has been reached. Alternatively, once the jam is boiling, use a digital thermometer to measure the temperature until it reaches 104°C, when the setting point is reached. Take the pan off the heat and leave for 10 minutes, then whisk the foam on the top back into the jam and pour into warmed, sterilized jars.

SALTED CARAMEL CUSTARD

Put the caster sugar into a heavy-based saucepan on a medium heat and let it dissolve slowly, then keep heating it until it becomes a dark brown caramel – this will take about 10 minutes. Don't let it go too far, or it will burn and become too bitter. Once the right colour is reached, stop the caramel cooking any further by taking the pan off the heat and adding the milk (watch out – it will spit and boil once the milk is added). Return it to a low heat and melt the caramel into the milk, stirring every few minutes.

Meanwhile, place the egg yolks, light brown sugar and 100g of the dark brown sugar in a large bowl and mix together for a few seconds, then sift in the flour and mix again.

Once the caramel has dissolved into the milk, bring to the boil and pour over the yolk mixture, whisking constantly to prevent curdling. Return this mixture to the saucepan and cook over a medium heat, whisking constantly for about 3–4 minutes, until very thick.

Pass through a fine sieve, then whisk in the salt. Place a sheet of cling film on the surface of the custard to prevent a skin from forming, leave to cool and then refrigerate.

Whip the cream and the remaining dark brown sugar together until thick, and fold into the chilled custard.

MAKES ENOUGH TO FILL 20 DOUGHNUTS GENEROUSLY

250g caster sugar

1 litre full fat milk

12 egg yolks

50g soft light brown sugar

150g soft dark brown sugar

90g plain white flour

1 teaspoon crunchy sea salt flakes

250ml double cream

SALTED HONEYCOMB

We use this honeycomb to top our caramel custard doughnuts. Makes lots, but you can never have enough – it's great sprinkled on ice cream or dipped in chocolate.

535g caster sugar

66g water

100g pure honey

186g liquid glucose

53g bicarbonate of soda

crunchy sea salt flakes

YOU WILL NEED

a kitchen thermometer

First, line your largest roasting tray with baking paper.

Put the sugar, water, honey and glucose into a large saucepan and stir together, then, on a medium heat, slowly let the sugar dissolve. Once dissolved, turn up the heat and bring to a rolling boil, then bring the temperature to 140°C. While it is coming up to temperature, make sure you have a large whisk handy, then sift the bicarbonate of soda into a small bowl and be poised ready for the mixture to reach the temperature.

What's going to happen is that once the sugar mixture reaches 140°C, you will add the bicarbonate of soda all at once and whisk into the boiling sugar. BE CAREFUL, as the mixture will be very hot. It will start to rise out of the saucepan, so as soon as you have whisked (we are talking seconds here), pour it into your lined baking tray, then put on a rack and leave to cool for 30 seconds before sprinkling on the salt.

Once it has cooled and hardened, go kung fu on it and break it into pieces. In a sealed jar it will keep for up to 2 months.

CORNFLAKE AND MALT CUSTARD

This is one of our favourite fillings for doughnuts, and any excuse to have a doughnut for breakfast!

Place the cornflakes in a plastic tub and pour over the milk. Cover, and place in the fridge overnight.

Next day, drain the milk into a saucepan, keeping the soggy cornflakes. Make sure you drain all the milk off – you should have at least 1 litre.

Preheat the oven to 120°C/fan 100°C/gas ½. Spread the soggy cornflakes thinly on a baking tray lined with baking paper and sprinkle with 20g of the demerara sugar. Put them into the oven for about 1½ hours, or until dry and crispy, then cool and store in an airtight container.

Slit the vanilla pod open lengthways and scrape out the seeds. Put the seeds and pod into a large saucepan along with the milk and the malt powder and bring slowly to the boil, to infuse the vanilla. Meanwhile, place the egg yolks, remaining 25g of demerara sugar, light brown sugar and 100g of caster sugar in a separate large bowl and mix for a few seconds, then sift in the flour and mix again.

Pour the boiling milk over the yolk mixture, whisking constantly to prevent curdling, then return the mixture to the pan and cook over a medium heat, whisking constantly for about 2 minutes, until very thick. Pass through a fine sieve, then place a sheet of cling film on the surface of the custard to prevent a skin forming.

Leave to cool, then refrigerate. Whip the cream with the malt syrup and the remaining 40g of caster sugar until thick, and fold into the chilled custard.

When you've filled your doughnuts to bursting, top each one with a fresh raspberry and sprinkle with the crispy cornflakes.

MAKES ENOUGH TO
FILL 20 DOUGHNUTS
GENEROUSLY

100g cornflakes

1.3 litres full fat milk

25g demerara sugar,
plus 20g for sprinkling

1 vanilla pod

40g malt powder

12 egg yolks

25g soft light brown
sugar

140g caster sugar

85g plain white flour

200ml double cream

2 tablespoons malt syrup

20 fresh raspberries

ORANGE AND CARDAMOM CUSTARD

Sometimes I (Justin) forget why there is so much fuss about my doughnuts, but when I made these for the first time, after a massive Friday night/Saturday morning shift at Bread Ahead and armed with a cup of tea and my new doughnut, I sat on the bench outside the bakery and devoured the doughnut, then, OMG, I remembered.

MAKES ENOUGH TO FILL 20 DOUGHNUTS GENEROUSLY

1 litre full fat milk

4 teaspoons ground cardamom

1 teaspoon crushed cardamom pods

zest of 6 oranges

12 egg yolks

175g caster sugar

75g plain white flour

250ml double cream

zest of 1 orange

Put the milk into a heavy-based saucepan with the ground and crushed cardamom and add the zest of 4 of the oranges. Bring slowly to the boil, to infuse the zest and cardamom.

Meanwhile, place the egg yolks in a bowl with 125g of the caster sugar and mix together for a few seconds, then sift in the flour and mix again.

Pour the boiling milk over the yolk mixture, whisking constantly to prevent curdling, then return the mixture to the pan. Cook over a medium heat, whisking constantly for about 3–4 minutes, until nice and thick. Pass through a fine sieve, then place a sheet of cling film on the surface of the custard to prevent a skin forming.

Leave to cool, then refrigerate.

Whip the cream, the zest of the fifth orange and the remaining 50g of caster sugar together until thick, then fold into the chilled custard.

Garnish your filled doughnuts with fine strips of orange peel from the remaining orange.

BAY LEAF CUSTARD AND APPLE

Peel and core the apples and chop them into small dice. Put them into a saucepan on a medium heat with 2 tablespoons of caster sugar, 3 bay leaves and the cider. Cook them until tender, then leave to cool.

Put the milk into a heavy-based saucepan, then scrunch up the rest of bay leaves and add to the pan. Place on a medium heat and slowly bring to boil, to infuse the bay.

Place the egg yolks and light brown sugar in a bowl with 100g of the caster sugar and mix together for a few seconds, then sift in the flour and mix again.

Pour the boiling milk over the yolk mixture, whisking constantly to prevent curdling, then return the mixture to the pan. Cook over a medium heat, whisking constantly for about 5 minutes, until very thick.

Pass through a fine sieve, then place a sheet of cling film on the surface of the custard to prevent a skin forming.

Leave to cool, then refrigerate.

Whip the cream and remaining 50g of caster sugar together until thick, then fold into the chilled custard.

Garnish your filled doughnuts with a bay leaf and a pile of cooked apple.

MAKES ENOUGH TO FILL
20 DOUGHNUTS
GENEROUSLY

4 crisp juicy eating apples

150g caster sugar, plus
2 tablespoons

10 fresh bay leaves, plus
more for garnish

50ml cider

1 litre full fat milk

12 egg yolks

50g soft light
brown sugar

75g plain white flour

250ml double cream

VELVET CHOCOLATE CUSTARD

1 litre full-fat milk

30g cocoa powder

12 egg yolks

145g caster sugar

70g plain white flour

150g plain chocolate
(70% or more), chopped
or buttons

250ml double cream

Put the milk and cocoa powder into a heavy-based saucepan and bring slowly to the boil to infuse the cocoa powder.

Meanwhile, place the egg yolks in a bowl with 120g of the caster sugar and mix together for a few seconds, then sift in the flour and mix again.

Pour the boiling milk over the yolk mixture, whisking constantly to prevent curdling, then return the mixture to the saucepan and add the chocolate. Cook over a medium heat, whisking constantly for around 3 minutes, until it's nice and thick and all the chocolate has dissolved into the custard.

Pass the custard through a fine sieve into a bowl and place a sheet of cling film on the surface to prevent a skin forming. Leave to cool, then refrigerate.

Whip the cream with the remaining 25g of caster sugar until thick and fold into the chilled custard.

Garnish your filled doughnuts with cocoa nibs or chopped chocolate, or some salted crispy pretzels for a little crunch. If feeling cheeky, try adding a few drops of rose or violet extract to the cream before whipping.

For a stunning chocolate and orange custard, add the zest of 2 oranges to the milk and cocoa, then continue with the recipe as above, adding a couple of drops of orange extract to the cream before whipping.

STOCKISTS

BREAD AHEAD
Proving baskets, scrapers,
aprons, baking books and
amazing baking classes.
www.breadahead.com
020 7403 5444

BOROUGH MARKET
Fresh and yummy produce, and the
home of Bread Ahead's Mothership
Bakery and Baking School.
www.boroughmarket.org.uk
020 7407 1002

EQUIPMENT

CRANE COOKWARE
Glorious and gorgeous cast-iron
pots for use as Dutch ovens.
www.cranecookware.com

JOSEPH JOSEPH
Sexy bakeware.
www.josephjoseph.com
Available nationwide in
good cook and kitchen shops.

LE CREUSET
Beautiful strong and
coloured cast-iron pots for
use as Dutch ovens.
www.lecreuset.co.uk
Available nationwide in good
cook and kitchen shops.

MIELE
The best ovens and fridges.
www.miele.co.uk
0330 160 6600

NISBETS
Professional
catering equipment.
www.nisbets.co.uk
0845 140 5555

SAINSBURY'S
Really good heavy-duty
bakeware which we use
in the baking school.
www.sainsburys.co.uk
Many stores around the UK.

SOUS CHEF
Pizza/bread peels.
www.souschef.co.uk
0800 270 7591

WILKO
Plastic bowls, wooden
spoons and scoops.
www.wilko.com
Many stores around the UK.

INGREDIENTS

DOVES FARM
Gluten-free flour.
www.dovesfarm.co.uk
01488 684880

HOLLAND AND BARRETT
Malt extract, coconut
flour, seeds and cereals.
www.hollandandbarrett.com
Many stores around the UK.
0370 606 6606

MARRIAGE'S
Lovely and happy flour
(which we use at
Bread Ahead).
www.flour.co.uk
01245 354455

OCADO
Fresh yeast.
www.ocado.com
0345 656 1234

RUDE HEALTH
Sprouted whole buckwheat flour
www.rudehealth.com
020 7731 3740

SPICE MOUNTAIN
Delicious spices.
www.spicemountain.co.uk
020 3609 3130

WHOLEFOODS
Gluten-free flours.
www.wholefoods.com

INDEX

THANKS

To all at Bread Ahead past and present, thank you for your passion and hard work.

To Juliet Annan, Anna Steadman and Alison O'Toole, a massive thank you, hugs and kisses for bringing our book to life.

To Issy Crocker for the MOST amazing pictures – you are a superstar! Thank you.

To Annie Lee, many thanks for finding all our mistakes and putting the book to rights.

To Al Richardson for the brilliant Lammas Day pictures.

To all our loyal customers, baking school students and wholesale clients, thank you for your ongoing support.

A big thank you to all our baking school teachers, especially Mr Chapman, who set things up at the beginning.

To Borough Market, for all their help and support since we opened in 2013.

To Southwark Cathedral, for the love and blessings and all the support with Lammas Day.

Chris Malec, thank you for steering the ship called Bread Ahead.

A real big up and thank you to Miele, for all the wonderful ovens in the baking school.

A big thanks to Joseph & Joseph for all the sexy bakeware for the baking school.

To Nick and all at Rude Health for the support and for the lovely flour.

To all our suppliers a thank you, especially to Marriage's for all those tons of happy flour.

To PG Tips, thank you for getting us through those long shifts.

To Ray, who brings sunshine to Saturday mornings.

To Nigella Lawson, thank you for all those tweets and retweets.

To Tom Kerridge, a big hug and thanks for putting us on the telly.

A big thanks to all our social media friends for supporting us from the beginning, especially @clerkenwell_boy and @ks_ate_here.

To our original superstar, Felicity Spector, thank you for all your support.

Oliver's bakery, thanks for being there when we run out of stuff, especially Chris.

Big thanks to Liza de Guia at food.curated. for the most incredible story and the support.

Tiff, big respect and thanks.

Gemma Bell and the team, big thanks for putting us out there.

Jan McCourt, thanks for being there in the hour of need.

And lastly to all the amazing people we have had the pleasure of working with over the years.